101 Careers *in* Gerontology

D1176992

101 Careers *in* Gerontology

C. Joanne Grabinski, MA, MA, ABD

SPRINGER PUBLISHING COMPANY

New York

Copyright © 2007 by Springer Publishing Company, LLC.

All rights reserved

No part of the publication may be reproduced, stored in a retrieval system, or transmitted in any form or by any means, electronic, mechanical, photocopying, recording, or otherwise, without the prior permission of Springer Publishing Company, LLC.

Springer Publishing Company, LLC.
11 West 42nd Street
New York, NY 10036
www.springerpub.com

Acquisitions Editor: Sheri W. Susman
Managing Editor: Mary Ann McLaughlin
Production Editor: Megan Timian
Cover Design: Joanne Honigman
Composition: Publication Services, Inc.

06 07 08 09 / 5 4 3 2 1

ISBN 978-0-8261-1506-5

Library of Congress Cataloging-in-Publication Data

Library of Congress Cataloging-in-Publication Data

Grabinski, C. Joanne, 1941-
   101 careers in gerontology / C. Joanne Grabinski.
      p. cm.
   ISBN 978-0-8261-1506-5 (pbk. : alk. paper)
   1. Gerontology—Vocational guidance—United States. 2. Older people—Services for—United States. I. Title. II. Title: One hundred one careers in gerontology.
   HQ1064.U5G66 2007
   305.2602373--dc22
                          2007028600

Printed in the United States of America by Bang Printing.

Dedication

In memory of Kristian Frederick Thomsen,
who unknowingly started me on my gerontology journey,
Mary Frances Gilbert
Fernande Pauline Eugenie Bouffioux Grabinski
Howard Y. McClusky
and in honor of
Elizabeth Oates Schuster
Mary Alice Wolf
Phoebe Liebig
who added stones to the path and have walked
with me along the way.

Contents

Author

C. Joanne Grabinski, MA, MA, ABD is President/Educator and Consultant for AgeEd in Mt. Pleasant, Michigan; Lecturer (1992-current), Gerontology Program at Eastern Michigan University in Ypsilanti, Michigan; and Adjunct Professor (1998-current), Human Development: Gerontology, at Saint Joseph College in West Hartford, Connecticut. She was Director and Assistant Professor (1984–1991), Interdisciplinary Gerontology Program at Central Michigan University in Mt. Pleasant, Michigan. She holds a BS in Home Economics Education from Oregon State University, MA degrees in Educational Administration: Community Leadership and in Family Relations from Central Michigan University, and completed doctoral work (ABD) in Family Ecology: Adult Development & Aging, with cognates in Gerontology and Sociology, at Michigan State University. Grabinski is the curriculum designer/professor of the first Introduction to Careers in Gerontology course in the United States. She has been actively involved in the Gerontological Society of America (GSA) and the Association for Gerontology in Higher Education (AGHE) for the past 27 years, serving on committees for both and as an elected member of the AGHE Executive Board, and is a long-standing member of the American Society on Aging (ASA). Grabinski is an AGHE Fellow in Gerontology and Geriatrics Education (awarded 1999), was an AGHE Distinguished Teacher (1997), and received an AGHE Part-Time Faculty Certificate of Recognition (2004).

Preface

As I began work on a master's degree in family relations and was trying to select the focus for my program of study, one of my professors advised me to look for the niches that were yet unfilled by academics and practitioners in the field. When I had a short list of such niches down on paper, she told me to pick one and make it mine. From that list I chose "aging," and my journey into the professional world of gerontology was off and running. Fast forward about 20 years and the director of the gerontology program at the university that is my academic "home" hired me to design another course—this time as a requirement for the undergraduate minor in gerontology. We had talked about this course for years and she felt the time was right to add it to the curriculum. The course is "Introduction to Careers in Gerontology," and I've had the privilege of teaching it for the past 6 years. About 3 years ago I was invited to write a chapter on "careers in aging" for a gerontology encyclopedia. Now, this book is a way to share with you many of the career paths and professional positions in the field of gerontology that I've learned about over the past 28 years. Some of these are well-established career options, some are just emerging, and others are possibilities just waiting for one or some of you to select as your niche in this ever expanding field of study, research, education, policy, and practice.

To help you explore career paths and positions in gerontology, this book intertwines career position profiles with interviews from individuals who currently hold some of these positions:

- Profiles: each profile includes the same categories of information so you can compare those you find interesting. In all, 68 profiles offer information about 100 possible career positions. Note that some profiles cover more than one position to allow you to consider variations in that position by the titles used and the certifications that create a "career ladder" within the position.
- Interviews: each of the 23 interviewees was asked the same questions, also for comparative purposes. Some of the interviewees respond from the perspective of only a year or two after earning their degrees. Others speak

from the perspective of greater career longevity within their career fields, although a few are new to the gerontological focus of their current positions. One has been in position for 20 years and another for 32 years.

In the closing section, . . . *and More*, you will find suggestions for positions in 25 different disciplines (e.g., anthropology, history, philosophy), professional fields (e.g., actuary, clothing and textiles, journalism, theatre arts), emerging subfields of gerontology (e.g., entrepreneurial gerontology, religious/spiritual gerontology), and, finally, some that are based in issues related to aging (e.g., elder abuse, neglect, and exploitation; exercise, fitness, and wellness; intimacy and sexuality; substance abuse and chemical dependency). For most of these, relevant professional organizations and Web sites are offered to allow further exploration. Overall, 142 possible career positions are suggested.

This book is written for all who are searching for a career niche that is a good fit. It is for college students trying to choose majors and minors, think about graduate school, or find their first job fresh out of college. It is for high school students thinking about what comes next and the guidance counselors (and, perhaps, parents) who are trying to help them make informed decisions about college majors and career path options. It is for persons of all ages, including older adults themselves, who want to start over in a new field after they have been downsized out of a job, experienced burnout in a current position, want to reenter the workforce after a time away, or want to work beyond retirement. Whatever your reasons for exploring career fields, this book is designed to provide you glimpses into, and information about, a broad range of options that are gerontology-specific or gerontology-related. Please note, however, that most of the positions presented in the book are "career positions," which means that most positions require at least an associate's or bachelor's degree. For some positions a master's degree is either required or preferred, and doctorates (academic or professional) are required for several positions. This allows the reader to consider entry-level jobs and to think about career paths that allow for continued growth and advancement across the course of one's career.

Although the actual writing of this book was mine alone to do, it could not have been done without the inspiration, support, and assistance of many others. Thank you, Leslie Lieberman (now deceased), for advising me to find my niche. Thank you, Elizabeth Schuster, co-creator of the idea for the careers in gerontology course, for allowing me the opportunity to bring the course to life and to teach it to others. To the students who have taken this course over the past 6 years, it is truly you who have made this book more interesting and useful than it would have been otherwise. It is a special joy that three of my former students agreed to be interviewees for the book. Special thanks goes to colleagues from around the country who recommended interviewees, answered questions about their career fields, and guided me to relevant resources so

I could broaden the scope of this book. To Debra Sheets and Phoebe Liebig, thank you beyond words for opening the door for me to do this book, and to Sheri Sussman at Springer, who listened to their recommendations, then mentored and guided me gently, with wisdom and laughter, through the ups and downs of authoring my first book. To my husband, Roger, my love, appreciation, and gratitude for encouraging and supporting me through the twisting paths of my nontraditional career journey, including the birth of this book.

Introduction

Wanted: gerontology workers, gerontological specialists, and gerontologists for careers now and into the future. Work with, for, and on behalf of the growing population of elders (including centenarians) in a wide variety of settings. Required: training/education in appropriate field and at appropriate level for specific position; specialization in aging studies/gerontology is highly desirable. Ability to rethink one's concept of old and deconstruct myths about old people and the processes of aging is mandatory. Compensation: income varies by specific type of position held; geographic location of employing agency, facility, or organization; education and experience background of applicant; and your willingness to risk getting involved with old people [try it—you might like it!]. Benefits: learn to grow old well yourself as you help to improve the quality of life for others who are aging.

Although this want ad will rarely appear among newspaper classified ads for employment or online career centers/job postings, it does speak to the growing number of career path options available now and in the future for persons interested in working with, for, and on behalf of the fastest growing segment of the U.S. population. Through the profiles of possible career positions, interviews with professionals in some of these career positions, and the . . . **and More** closing section, it is the purpose of this book to give you a taste of the wide variety of career paths that are open for someone interested in a career in gerontology and to identify sources of further information about career positions that you find interesting.

WHAT IS GERONTOLOGY?

From an academic perspective, *gerontology* is the study of the biological, psychological, and sociological aspects of aging. Some academicians recognize gerontology as a discipline or multidisciplinary field of study that draws upon the expertise of many disciplines. Others view gerontology as an interdisciplinary field in which two or more disciplines are intertwined to offer more complex insights and understandings about the processes of aging and the elderly population than can be gained through work in just one discipline. Regardless of one's perspective, the three base disciplines for the field are biology, psychology, and sociology, as is reflected in the design of gerontology education programs in higher education. Also, the first gerontological researchers emerged out of these disciplines. Over time, more disciplines (for example, history, anthropology, religion, political science, philosophy) have become involved in gerontology education and research. Among the more recent disciplines to step into the gerontology arena are from the humanities and arts (such as literature, language arts, communication, visual arts), which is being recognized by the establishment of a new professional journal on aging, humanities and the arts.

From a professional perspective, medicine, nursing, clinical psychology, and social work were among the first professions to develop aging-specific education and practice orientations to meet the needs of a client base with increasing numbers of older adults. Today, many other professions—law; occupational, physical, art, and music therapy; home economics/human ecology; nutrition and dietetics; interior design and architecture; business; education; technology and engineering; health administration; and public administration—are entering this realm of research, education, and practice. As the academic study of gerontology and the professional field on aging have expanded, gerontology has become the overarching "umbrella" for an ever-expanding number of subfields, including geriatric medicine and dentistry, gerontological social work and nursing, and clinical geropsychology. Among the newer specializations are educational gerontology, policy and aging, elder law, financial gerontology, geriatric pharmacy, family gerontology, intergenerational studies, and spiritual gerontology.

WHAT CREATED THE INTEREST IN GERONTOLOGY AS A FIELD OF STUDY AND AS A PROFESSION?

Why this increasing interest in aging research? What has influenced so many disciplinary and professional fields of study to incorporate gerontology as part of their discipline-based educational and training programs? What is behind the growth and diversity of career paths related to aging/gerontology? It appears that four factors have been of prime importance:

- Enactment of aging-specific federal legislation, beginning with the Social Security Act in 1935, and, more significantly, the Older Americans Act (OAA) in 1965 that established what is known as the "formal aging network"—a hierarchical system that includes the Administration on Aging

(AoA) at the federal level, state units on aging (such as an Office of Services to the Aging or a Department of Aging), Area Agencies on Aging (AAAs) at the regional level within states, and direct service agencies (such as county commissions, departments, and bureaus on aging) at the county level. With each OAA reauthorization, new types of programs and services are added to meet newly assessed needs of elders.

- Growth in the actual numbers of persons who are 65 years of age and older and in the proportion of the total U.S. population that consists of older adults.
- Development of gerontology and geriatrics education programs at institutions of higher education. At the present time, more than 500 institutions of higher education (community colleges, colleges, universities, professional schools) offer degree components (concentrations, specializations, minors, cognates, certificates) or majors and degrees in gerontology. Further information about these programs is available in two resources of the Association for Gerontology in Higher Education (AGHE): the *Directory of Educational Programs in Gerontology and Geriatrics* (Stepp, 2007) and a computer search service of its *Database of Educational Programs in Gerontology and Geriatrics.** AGHE developed curriculum standards and guidelines for gerontology programs at each academic level and for each type of credential. Programs that fulfill the standards are eligible to apply for "Program of Merit" status. Four core courses (Introduction to Gerontology/ Social Gerontology, Biology/Physiology/Health Aspects of Aging, Psychology of Aging, and Sociology of Aging) and a practicum or field experience are commonly required in formal gerontology education programs. Students also have an opportunity to select gerontology elective courses (e.g., on policy, family relationships, nutrition, religion/spirituality, gender, economics, sexuality, recreation, interior design, humanities and the arts, death and dying) that fit the student's professional and personal interests. These standards and guidelines, however, are voluntary and intentionally flexible to allow administrators and faculty on each campus to tailor their programs to fit the unique needs, style, and environment at each institution.
- Creation of gerontology professional organizations, including the Gerontological Society of America (GSA), the Association for Gerontology in Higher Education (AGHE), the American Society on Aging (ASA), and the National Council on Aging (NCOA). In addition to these national level organizations, a number of regional and state professional organizations have been formed. Many other professional organizations have member sections specific to aging/gerontology (such as the American Psychological Association's Division 20 on Adult Development and Aging or the American Sociological Association's Aging and the Life Course section).

WHAT IS A GERONTOLOGIST?

Until recently that has been a difficult question to answer. A proposed schema, however, now makes it possible to organize those who work with and/or on behalf of elders into three categories:

- *Gerontology workers* have no formal gerontology education or training even though they work directly with or on behalf of elderly clients or in an aging-specific organization or facility. They may work in paraprofessional roles (such as certified nurse assistants in a nursing home or a receptionist for a county commission on aging) or as professionals who are fully credentialed in fields other than gerontology (such as social workers who are discharge planners in a hospital or a family practice physician whose practice in a rural medical clinic includes many elderly patients).
- *Gerontological specialists* have completed at least one degree in a discipline or professional field that is not gerontology-specific, but included a formal gerontology degree component (e.g., minor, certificate, cognate, or specialization in gerontology), or they obtained specialized postgraduate gerontology training (perhaps through a freestanding credit or noncredit certificate program in gerontology; a profession-specific certification or registration process; continuing education coursework, workshops, or other training programs; or a postdoctoral fellowship) that complements or enhances the field of study in which they received their degree(s). For example, an interior designer-gerontological specialization holds a degree with a major in interior design and a minor or cognate in gerontology; a director of an older adult library program has a degree in library science to which gerontology expertise has been added through participation in a summer institute on lifelong libraries and completion of an online certificate in gerontology; and a recreational, occupational, or physical therapist obtains gerontology/geriatric certification according to standards set by relevant professional organizations and/or their accrediting bodies.
- *Gerontologists* have earned degrees for which gerontology was the primary, not secondary, field of study. This relatively new category of gerontology professionals is the result of an increasing number of degree programs in gerontology, aging studies, or a similarly titled degree label. By 2005 approximately 126 gerontology-specific degree programs were in existence (18 associate, 41 bachelor's, 58 master's, and 9 doctoral).

Currently, it appears that the majority of gerontology-specific and -related paraprofessional and professional positions are held by persons who are either gerontology workers or gerontology specialists. This is changing as more persons complete formal gerontology education , so for the purposes of this book, the career position profiles and interviews focus on professionals who are gerontological specialists and/or gerontologists. While this delineation of three types of career positions in gerontology is helpful in thinking about where you might fit in this growing professional field, please keep in mind that this schema is not yet commonly used by either educators or employers.

WHAT TYPES OF JOBS ARE AVAILABLE IN GERONTOLOGY?

According to Peterson, Douglass, and Lobenstine Whittington (2004), seven types of job roles exist for gerontological specialists and this role delineation also works well for gerontologists:

- Advocate
- Direct service provider
- Educator/trainer
- Manager/administrator
- Marketer and product developer
- Program planner and evaluator
- Researcher

Each of these roles is represented among the career position profiles and interviews in this book. Although this listing is not intended to be hierarchical, you may find it useful in prioritizing the type of job roles that do or do not interest you. Keep in mind also that many professionals carry out two or more of these roles, with equal or equitable attention to each, as they fulfill their job responsibilities. Finally, some job roles, such as recruiter and counselor/advisor, are not visible in this listing, so it should not be seen as exhaustive of all job roles that exist or are possible.

WHERE DO GERONTOLOGICAL SPECIALISTS AND GERONTOLOGISTS WORK?

The array of specific places where gerontological specialists and gerontologists are employed is too extensive to list here, although it is possible to suggest what the most common types of work settings are:

- Educational settings (public and private): community and junior colleges, 4-year colleges, universities, technical/vocational and professional schools, seminaries; community and professional organizations, programs, and foundations that focus on aging and provide educational programs and services for older adults; adult education and older learner programs; libraries and information centers; employee training/education divisions in industry and corporate settings; patient education services in medical centers/clinics; and community-based agencies related to physical and mental health

- Organizations: professional organization conference management and training programs; chronic disease/disorders organizations, associations, and foundations; race/ethnicity-specific councils on aging; gender-specific organizations and initiatives; membership organizations for older persons
- Medical care, rehabilitation and residential settings: long-term care and assisted living centers; hospitals/medical centers; mental health facilities; VA hospitals; private practice; rehabilitation centers; in-home care agencies and services; private practice
- Residential communities and facilities: retirement communities, senior living residences; kinship care housing centers; corrections facilities; co-housing for elders
- Religious and spiritual settings: churches, synagogues, mosques; religious retreat centers; interfaith/interdenominational organizations; faith-based outreach programs
- Governmental agencies: county commissions, divisions, or bureaus on aging; Area Agencies on Aging; state aging services offices and departments; federal Administration on Aging; Social Security Administration offices; Medicare and Medicaid service centers and assistance programs; prescription assistance and counseling programs; public health departments; National Institutes of Health, including National Institute on Aging
- Corporate, industry, and business settings: banks, financial planning firms and services; investment firms and brokerages; law firms and legal assistance services; insurance industry; retail stores and chains; restaurant and hotel chains; trade associations and unions; manufacturing firms
- Self-employment

As with the listing of job roles, this listing is not exhaustive. Please note that each career position profile includes a listing of common and potential workplace(s).

CAREER POSITION PROFILES AND INTERVIEWS

The array of career paths and professional positions open to gerontological specialists and gerontologists is almost limitless. While some positions are well-established in traditional fields (such as social work, nursing, occupational and physical therapy, dietetics, audiology, speech-language pathology, recreational therapy), other positions are in traditional fields with a relatively recent focus on gerontology (such as elder law, clinical geropsychology, geriatric medicine, architecture, gerontological/geriatric optometry, interior design-gerontology specialization and healthcare interior design, geriatric and senior care pharmacy). Gerontology is also a "growth industry" as many new career paths and position opportunities emerge from new sub-fields of gerontology (like financial gerontology, family gerontology, and religious/spiritual gerontology); as new positions evolve within disciplines and professions that already integrate gerontology into their educational and training programs; and as more disciplines and professions forge new linkages with gerontology. The profiles and interviews presented in this book are intended to give you a "taste" from each of these three perspectives. By presenting the same type of information in each profile and asking the same questions of each interviewee, you will be able to do some "comparison shopping." At the end of each profile is a brief listing of key professional organizations and Web sites to help you explore further those positions that intrigue you.

. . . AND MORE

In this section of the book, you will find additional listings of even more career paths and positions that can be linked to gerontology, although the linkages may be so newly forged that there is little or no information available about them or the linkages are not yet clearly visible. They are listed, however, to tweak your interest, spur your imagination, and help you identify a broader spectrum of career possibilities that might be a good fit for you. When possible, a relevant professional organization, Web site, or other information is provided. Welcome to the exciting, dynamic, and ever-expanding professional world of gerontology!

REFERENCES

Peterson, D. A., Douglass, E. B., & Lobenstine Whittington, J. (2004). *Careers in aging: Opportunities and options.* Washington, DC: Association for Gerontology in Higher Education.
Stepp, D. D. (2007). *Directory of educational programs in gerontology and geriatrics* (8th ed.). Washington, DC: Association for Gerontology in Higher Education.

---

*For further information about use of the AGHE *Database of Educational Programs in Gerontology and Geriatrics*, contact AGHE at info@aghe.org.

Actuary

Basic Description: Actuary is all about "risk"—the possibility that something undesirable will occur. Actuaries assess the likelihood that risk will occur in the future, design strategies to avoid or prevent risk, measure incidents of and factors related to the occurrence of undesirable events, attempt to reduce the potential for risk, and work to reduce the impact of the undesirable events that do occur. They are key players in the design of programs and products that control and manage risk through their work in one of the four major actuarial areas: life insurance, property and casualty insurance, pensions, and health. Actuary was identified as one of the 25 best careers for 2007 by *U.S. News and World Report*.

Education and Experience Requirements: A bachelor's degree in business, math, finance, actuarial science, economics, liberal arts, or related fields, and a strong math background is essential. Coursework in communications (e.g., writing, technical writing, speech, drama), literature, history, art, political science, the humanities, and other social sciences is recommended. Beyond the bachelor's degree, becoming an actuary is based on earning one or more of three professional designations (Associate, Fellow, Enrolled Actuary) acquired through an actuarial organization, and gaining status through the professional examination system. Designation candidates must pass a series of tests at each level.

Certification, Licensure, and Continuing Education Requirements: Licensure to become an Enrolled Actuary is granted by a joint board of the Department of Treasury and the Department of Labor. Licensure is mandatory in order to perform actuarial tasks required for pension plans.

Core Competencies and Skills Needed:
- Specialized math knowledge (calculus, linear algebra, statistics, probability)
- Keen analytical, project management, and problem-solving skills
- Good business sense regarding finance, accounting, marketing, and economics
- Solid oral and written communication skills
- Strong computer skills, including word-processing programs, spreadsheets, statistical analysis programs, database manipulation, and programming languages

- A joy of learning; interested in a variety of historical, social, legislative, and political issues
- Ambition; self-motivation
- Creativity

Compensation: This varies by one's status in the national examination system, designation level, licensure, type of professional specialty, and nature of the employment setting.

Workplace(s): These include the financial services sector (such as insurance companies, commercial banks, investment banks and firms, retirement fund companies), corporations, state and federal government agencies, consulting firms, and self-employed private practice.

Employment Outlook: Good.

Related Professional Organizations and Web Sites:

- Be An Actuary: www.beanactuary.org
- American Academy of Actuaries (AAA): www.actuary.org
- American Society of Pension Actuaries (ASPA): www.aspa.org
- Casualty Actuarial Society (CAS): www.casact.org
- Conference of Consulting Actuaries (CCA): www.ccactuaries.org
- Society of Actuaries (SOA): www.soa.org

Adult Day Program Coordinator

Basic Description: Adult day program coordinators plan for and provide daily care at an adult day program center for adults over the age of 60 who are experiencing temporary or progressive memory loss due to dementia or other causes. Adult day program coordinators plan and supervise activities that are appropriate to the age, physical health, and mental health status of program attendees. They conduct home visits to assess the needs of clients and caregivers, develop follow-up plans for caregivers, and facilitate educational programs and support groups As coordinators, they schedule and supervise day care staff. They also recruit, train, and schedule volunteers, then coordinate and supervise volunteer interaction with program clients.

Education and Experience Requirements: A bachelor's or master's degree in social work, clinical psychology, occupational therapy, or therapeutic recreation is required; gerontology (either as coursework or a degree component) is strongly recommended.

Certification, Licensure, and Continuing Education Requirements: These vary by place of employment, state licensing requirements, and professional field.

Core Competencies and Skills Needed:

- Ability to work with older adults from diverse ethnic, racial, cultural, and socioeconomic backgrounds
- Respect for cultures other than your own
- Good written and oral communication skills; attentive listener
- Ability to design activity plans for clients with varying levels of cognitive functioning
- Creativity in planning activities for persons with memory loss and/or dementia
- Ability to quickly mediate problems that occur with day program clients
- Good organizational skills
- Good staff and volunteer coordination and supervision skills
- Patience and a sense of humor

Compensation: This varies by education, experience, nature of employment setting, level of responsibility, and geographical location.

Workplace(s): These include health care systems, medical centers, long-term care and skilled nursing facilities, community mental health agencies, multi-service organizations serving older adults, and freestanding day care facilities funded by community or faith-based organizations.

Employment Outlook: Moderate to high—depending on geographical location.

Related Professional Organizations and Web Sites:

- National Adult Day Services Association (NADSA): www.nadsa.org

An Interview with
Patricia Lee Hall,
Adult Day Program Coordinator,
University-Based Hospital System

What is your educational background in gerontology and other disciplines or professional fields? What formal credentials (e.g., completed degrees, certification) do you hold in these fields?

Currently I have a Bachelor's of Social Work (BSW) degree and a Graduate Certificate in Gerontology-Dementia. In 2008, I will receive my Master's of Social Work degree (MSW). I am a member of the Gerontological Society of America (GSA) and National Association of Social Workers (NASW).

Briefly describe your gerontology-related career path.

For the past seven years I have worked as a program coordinator for the adult day club in the health care system of a major university. The club is an adult day program for people 60 and older with memory loss. We provide a wide array of activities and social stimulation for people who attend the adult day program. After receiving my MSW, it is my desire to provide counseling support services to the caregivers of the families we serve.

How did you first become interested in your current professional position?

I had an extended family member who had polio. My sisters and I would work for her to earn extra money. Working with her taught us to be patient and compassionate towards someone who was less fortunate. As a child, I also remember having grandparents who were an intricate part of our lives. I learned at a very young age that the older generation had much wisdom and knowledge. They had experienced things I hoped I would never have to go through. I loved to listen to them tell me about their difficult times. I learned how to be compassionate at a very young age.

What are the most rewarding aspects of your career?

The most rewarding aspect of my job is serving the club members we serve. Seeing them take part in the activities that are provided, regardless of whether they are able to complete the entire activity, and seeing them take pride in their accomplishment, no matter how big or small, is rewarding.

What are the most challenging aspects of your career?

The club program membership is comprised predominantly of females. One of our biggest challenges in the program is finding activities that the men who attend the program enjoy and don't find demeaning. Another challenge is finding activities for the different cognitive levels of the silver club members. It is my wish that we be able to find activities that everyone can take pride in and enjoy.

Describe a typical workday in your current professional position.

Staff arrives an hour before members to arrange the flow of the day. When members arrive at the club, coffee and toast is served and each member has an opportunity to talk with those sitting near them. Next, we plan several activities for the morning. These vary but include such things as: singing as a whole group with a volunteer pianist, Bible study with a local pastor volunteer, art with varied mediums, and, always, physical fitness, which is done with members sitting on chairs. We serve lunch daily at the same time and, most often, in the same way. We find members appreciate that the schedule remains constant for basic activities. The afternoon may include working with a professional music therapist or special gardening projects with local master gardeners who may have volunteered or, perhaps, with our own staff. We often have a group baking a yummy treat earlier in the day that can be enjoyed before our members leave for the day. The final two hours of the day, after the members have left, is filled with required paperwork and the necessary clean up.

How do you balance career and other aspects of your life?

As with everyone today, my life is very busy. I have graduate school, church (where I love to sing), community service organizations that I participate in, and my work at the adult day program club to fit into my days. The club, however, has an outstanding feature built into its employment—an "office day."

One day of the week I am not on the floor; instead, I am able to take care of phone calls, documentation, and planning for the remainder of the week. This is a wonderful opportunity to "get caught up." When the time comes to either move on to another position or begin my own program, I will be sure to include an office day for my employees or to insist that office time be part of my benefits plan.

What advice do you have for someone contemplating a career in gerontology? In a professional position similar to your current position?

Love the old!

Advocate

Basic Description: Advocates inform target audiences, including elders, about relevant issues of concern. They also actively work with and/or on behalf of elders to raise awareness about needs and appropriate responses to those needs and to create policy that responds to identified needs. They may participate directly or indirectly in the enactment of public and/or private policy. In some cases they represent their older adult constituency; in others, they assist and support older adults to speak and act for themselves. They fulfill their job responsibilities through a variety of roles, such as educator, facilitator, spokesperson, policy watcher, policy analyst, policy developer, and policy opponent or proponent.

Education and Experience Requirements: A bachelor's degree or higher in public administration, sociology, applied sociology, social work or a graduate degree in public policy, law, or policy and aging is preferred. Gerontology coursework or a degree component is strongly recommended.

Certification, Licensure, and Continuing Education Requirements: Advocates must meet requirements related to practice in a specific professional field, state or governmental jurisdiction, or employing agency.

Core Competencies and Skills Needed:
- Policy analysis and policy development skills
- Advocacy skills
- Competence at building and maintain networks
- Public speaking skills
- Excellent written and oral communication skills
- Working knowledge of coalition-building processes and techniques
- Working knowledge of grassroots organizational process and techniques
- Ability to multitask
- Diplomacy; willingness and ability to work successfully within governmental protocol

Compensation: This varies by one's education, experience, the nature of the employing organization/agency, the type and level of the position within the organizational hierarchy, and the geographic location.

Workplace(s): These include national and international advocacy organizations; federal, state, or local level grassroots organizations; lobbying groups; and an independent or consulting practice as an advocate, organizer, or lobbyist.

Employment Outlook: Good—especially with the anticipated growth of the older adult population over the next few decades.

Related Professional Organizations and Web Sites:

- AARP National Legal Training Project (NTLP): http://aarpnltp.grovesite. com
- Center for Medicare Advocacy: www.medicareadvocacy.org and www. fairmedicare.org
- National Senior Citizens Law Center (NSCLC): www.nsclc.org

An Interview with
Morgan F. Gable,
Assistant Director of Grassroots
Advocacy, International
Organization

What is your educational background in gerontology and other disciplines or professional fields? What formal credentials (e.g., completed degrees, certification) do you hold in these fields?

I spent most of my time in higher education studying how to work with older adults. While receiving my Bachelor of Social Work (BSW) degree, I did obtain generalist social work skills, but I chose to specialize with older adults very early in my career. I also earned a Certificate in Gerontology. In the graduate work for my Master's in Social Work (MSW) degree, I again specialized in working with older adults. I was trained in Community Organizing, with a minor in Human Services Management for Aging/Older Adults, and certified as a Specialist in Aging. Also, I was awarded designation as a McGregor Geriatric Social Work Fellow. After earning my master's degree, I was selected to be an Association for Gerontology in Higher Education (AGHE) intern for one semester.

Briefly describe your gerontology-related career path.

I first became interested in working with older adults when my grandmother first began to develop signs of Parkinson's disease. She and I had always been incredibly close, but when my mother and I took care of her for the last five years of her life, after she was no longer able to live alone, was when I officially decided that the world of gerontology was the field for me. The wisdom and experiences that I gained from those five years truly helped mold my future career path and I thank her for that everyday!

How did you first become interested in your current professional position?

I always wanted to work with older adults, but from a macro level. I never wanted to work in a clinical situation where I would have a caseload. Instead, I wanted to work on issues that affect older adults in terms of federal legislation and advocacy efforts. My current position is great because I am able to track—and advocate for changes to—federal legislation (e.g., Medicare Part D and Social Security issues) that has a direct impact on older adults in the United States. Working with a membership organization like this, however, has also given me the chance to work directly with some older adults. For example, I get to interact from a macro perspective in planning our programming across the country, but also from a micro perspective when I travel to these areas and get the chance to talk with (and learn from!) our many older adult attendees!

What are the most rewarding aspects of your career?

The most rewarding aspect of my career is knowing that I am (in some small way) bettering the lives of older adults. While I rarely get to witness firsthand the impact of the work that I do on behalf of older people, I am able to realize the tremendous effect that policy work has on the lives of all people. When I am able to act as an effective advocate (for example when we are successful in obtaining additional funding for Older Americans Act programs), I know that somewhere, someone will have a better life as a result of our efforts.

What are the most challenging aspects of your career?

The most challenging aspect of my job involves the "politics" and bureaucracy that I encounter when working with other coalitions and when working with the federal government. Sometimes I get frustrated about the "red tape" and the "political correctness" that one must deal with when engaging in advocacy work that seeks to change federal legislation. For example, it is hard for me to understand why the funding of stem cell research is such a controversial debate when I speak to our members who could someday benefit greatly from this innovative form of research.

Describe a typical workday in your current professional position.

As most in this field would say, there is no "typical" day. Most days, I research pending legislation and track the congressional votes (e.g., how each congressperson is voting). I also try to engage our members and supporters in our efforts by showing them how federal legislation has an impact on their daily lives and how they play a key role in producing change at every level of the government. Recently, I have been involved in coordinating programs across that country that seek to educate older adults about the multitude of services that are available in the United States.

How do you balance career and other aspects of your life?

Since it is early on in my career, I have really tried to "throw" myself into my career right now, although I also try to keep a clear perspective about my priorities in life. My family and friends are incredibly important and, while they realize that I really value my career, they help me balance them both by being both supportive and understanding.

What advice do you have for someone contemplating a career in gerontology? In a professional position similar to your current position?

The key to obtaining a position similar to mine is networking! The "aging" professional world is incredibly small and the "aging" policy/advocacy world is even smaller. It's a great group of people, but getting a position within the group is competitive, especially coming right out of school. The key for me was to first get my foot in the door by obtaining an internship. Through this internship, I was able to work my way into this group. I attended key coalition meetings where the many leaders of the policy and advocacy world came together. By learning and observing how they operated and what issues they were working on, I was able to gain an advantage over other applicants looking for a policy/advocacy position working on behalf of older adults. This also gave me the opportunity to receive job postings and "inside" information about upcoming openings for positions. Without my internship, I doubt that I would have been able to ever break into the policy/advocacy world in the field of aging.

Aging & Adult Services Division Manager, County Department of Human Services

Basic Description: A division manager is a position located between case-workers/case supervisors and division directors in county departments of human services; it is the first step into an administrative position within the agency. The line of report is to the aging and adult services division director in larger counties or directly to the top agency administrator in smaller counties. Division managers plan, organize, train, and review the work of division supervisors and/or case-workers, clerical and support staff, and other agency staff members responsible for some aspect of aging and adult services. They also advise their staff members on agency policies, procedures, fiscal matters, and program development or changes. It is their responsibility to ensure that agency standards, criteria, and other county, state, and federal regulations are maintained.

Educational and Experience Requirements: A master's degree in social work, gerontology, or a closely related field from an accredited institution of higher education required and additional coursework or a degree component in gerontology is strongly recommended (if the master's degree major is not gerontology-specific). Coursework and training in organizational management and personnel administration is encouraged. Also, a candidate for this position needs a minimum of four years full-time (of which two years must have been at the supervisory or management level for adult programs) social casework experience with elders and/or a vulnerable adult population in a public or private social welfare agency.

Certification, Licensure, and Continuing Education Requirements: Aging & adult services division managers must meet licensure requirements in the state where the practice occurs, along with the continuing education requirements of the employing agency.

Core Competencies and Skills Needed:

- Working knowledge of human service and aging-related service regulations at the county, state, and federal level

- Working knowledge of services and program development processes
- Commitment to the mission of the agency and the division
- Staff development and personnel administration skills
- Excellent written and oral communication skills
- Ability to work collaboratively with administrators in other divisions of the agency
- Commitment to legal and ethical professional practice

Compensation: This varies by one's education, experience, the level of the position within agency, and geographical location.

Workplace(s): This is specifically the county department of human services.

Employment Outlook: Fair—but improving as larger county departments of human services experience increased demands for adult/aging services as the population of elders grows rapidly over the next 2 decades. Opportunities for promotion to division director are limited (positions usually become open when current division directors retire), and are based on competitive examination results and other promotion criteria.

Related Professional Organizations and Web Sites:
None have yet been identified.

Alzheimer's Association Chapter Program Director

Basic Description: A program director for an Alzheimer's Association chapter at the state, regional, or local level is responsible for oversight of programs and services to educate and support families of persons with Alzheimer's disease and related conditions in the service area of the chapter for which they work. Program directors oversee chapter staff members and volunteers in the delivery of quality programs and services that meet chapter standards and are consistent with the mission of the Alzheimer's Association. Although the particular mix of job functions and the percentage of time devoted to each function will vary from one chapter to another, the following is a composite sample of responsibilities based on several job postings for this position:

- Program delivery (35%): oversee of Helpline and Care Consultation programs and services, including recruitment, training, and supervision of Helpline volunteers; provide direct education and support services for families and family caregivers (including information about resources, educational programs, care consultation, and support group referrals); oversee, expand, and evaluate support group programming; supervise, train, and nurture program volunteers; build a strong volunteer base; collect quantitative and qualitative data for program evaluation and reporting purposes; develop and expand the chapter's library and resource center
- Education programs (30%): plan and implement training programs (including packaged Alzheimer's Association programs such as Understanding Memory Loss, Savvy Caregiver, and Training for Dignity); deliver presentations at conferences, seminars and workshops for families, professionals, and related audiences; assist chapter director in the development of an annual educational conference for professionals in the chapter service area; coordinate volunteers for the chapter's Speaker's Bureau
- Public awareness (20%): establish new linkages and expand existing partnerships with local, regional, or state health/mental health agencies, relevant community-based organizations, and appropriate government entities; assist the chapter director in expanding revenues, increasing public awareness of chapter/association fundraising events and other activities; direct work with newsletter editor to develop educational themes and caregiver information for the chapter newsletter
- Multicultural outreach (10%): assist the chapter director and other staff to meet strategic goals related to outreach and service to diverse cultural and ethnic communities within the chapter's service area
- Administration (5%): assist chapter director to assure adequate staff and office coverage for chapter programs and services, and provision of oversight for office administration, including office staff and volunteers

Education and Experience Requirements: A bachelor's degree or higher in a health-related field is required; a master's degree is preferred for state-level positions. At least 3–5 years of relevant work experience in an Alzheimer's-specific setting (especially in counseling Alzheimer's patients and their families) is required and should include evidence of working in the community to conduct outreach, cultivate contacts, and establish collaborative relationships. An educational background in gerontology with a focus on dementia is desirable.

Certification, Licensure, and Continuing Education Requirements: Chapter program directors must meet relevant state licensure mandates and employing agency requirements for certification. Participation in continuing education programs, including attendance at the national Alzheimer's Association educational conference, is encouraged.

Core Competencies and Skills Needed:

- Ability to work with caregiving families to meet their needs (such as dealing with caregiver stress or coping with difficult behaviors)
- Demonstrated management skills, including personnel supervision
- Strong public speaking and presentation skills
- Excellent organizational and project management skills
- Knowledge of community and external services, programs, organizations, and other resources that support persons with dementia and their families
- Computer skills related to word processing, database, and graphics software
- Bilingual skills desirable in some locations
- Self-starter; willing to take initiative and work without supervision
- Available for and willing to work evenings, weekends, and holidays
- Ability and willingness to travel throughout region or state, as needed, for work-related purposes
- Ability to handle problems in a direct, firm, and caring manner

Compensation: This depends on one's education and experience. It may vary by geographical location and whether the position is at the state or regional level.

Workplace(s): These are the state and regional Alzheimer's Association chapter offices (some chapters have multiple local offices).

Employment Outlook: Good.

Related Professional Organizations and Web Sites:
Alzheimer's Association: www.alz.org [see job postings on chapter Web sites]

Applied Sociologist
Clinical Sociologist

Basic Description: Sociology is concerned with the understanding of groups or populations, such as the older adult population or its subgroups. **Applied Sociologists** use sociological knowledge to understand current problems or issues and their solutions for populations. When the population of interest is the elderly population, applied sociologists use their knowledge to make informed policy decisions and effectively manage or administer the programs for which they are responsible. Although they may help shape research efforts, they are more often consumers, rather than conductors, of research. Problems and issues they address might include law enforcement, housing, homelessness, transportation, community relations, corporate hiring strategies, health care, education, or other societal problems directly related to their focus on elders. **Clinical Sociologists**, by contrast, apply sociological knowledge through actual intervention; they use sociological techniques to guide the process of change in a wide variety of social settings. While they sometimes intervene with or on behalf of an individual, they are more likely to work with or through groups such as elders and their families, support networks or agencies, organizations, and corporations at the community, state, federal, and international level. Their "toolkit" of expertise includes skills related to counseling, mediation and conflict resolution, assessment, evaluation, and facilitation.

Education and Experience Requirements: A bachelor's degree in sociology or applied sociology is a minimum requirement; a graduate degree in sociology, applied sociology, demography, criminology, social gerontology, or another subfield of sociology is required for many clinical or applied practice positions (e.g., therapists, counselors, agency directors, researchers, statisticians). Gerontology coursework or a degree component is also strongly recommended.

Certification, Licensure, and Continuing Education Requirements: Clinical sociologists must meet state licensure requirements, if any, in order to conduct a clinical practice.

Core Competencies and Skills Needed:

- Good working knowledge of the processes and tools used in research, assessment, evaluation, problem-solving, conflict resolution, and policy analysis, development, and enactment
- Excellent written and oral communication skills
- Ability to think through problems, issues, and concerns at the societal level
- Good working knowledge of organization structure and function
- Familiarity with market analysis and focus group techniques

Compensation: This varies by education, experience, the nature of the employment setting, the level of responsibility, and geographical location.

Workplace(s): These include social service agencies and corporate, nonprofit, and governmental settings.

Employment Outlook: Promising—but difficult to track since relevant positions may be filled by professionals from other applied and clinical fields (such as clinical psychology and social work).

Related Professional Organizations and Web Sites:
* American Sociological Association (ASA): www.asanet.org [see ASA Sociological Practice Section for further information]

Architect

Basic Description: A growing sector of the professional field of architecture is devoted to designing home environments that support and aid normal changes in human and family function that occur with aging (including original design, renovation, remodeling, aging-in-place planning, consumer-created cooperatives, and co-housing projects); residential and long-term care facilities that adapt to the changing needs of elders who are physically and/or mentally frail, (e.g., continuing care residential communities, assisted living and skilled nursing facilities, adult day program centers, and memory care and dementia care settings); and community-based activity centers that serve older adults (e.g., senior centers, wellness therapy, and fitness centers). Tasks for which architects are responsible include site analysis; interviews and questionnaires with intended residents and, for facilities, also with staff members; architectural design and documentation; interior architectural planning and design; structural, mechanical, and electrical engineering (along with consultants); construction administration and oversight; and post-occupancy evaluation. For multiunit projects and multiperson residential and care facilities, additional tasks include project architectural research, strategic master planning, strategic program and environment redefinition, project conception and pro forma development (along with consultants), project development, and capital campaign collateral development.

Education and Experience equirements: A minimum of a Bachelor of Architecture (BArch) degree, which is a 5 year first professional degree, is required. A Master of Architecture (MArch) degree is strongly recommended, and may be earned by completing one of two optional paths: (1) a 4 year preprofessional degree (BA or BS) plus a 2 year professional architecture degree program or (2) a 4 year nonarchitecture degree (BA or BS in another field) plus a 3–4 year Master of Architecture (MArch) degree. Gerontology coursework or a degree component is recommended.

Certification, Licensure, and Continuing Education Requirements: Architects must comply with the licensure and registration requirements in the state where the practice occurs. Most states require a postgraduate training period (usually 3 years) under the direct supervision of a licensed architect in order to become eligible to take the Architect Registration Exam. Registered architects are eligible for certification by the National Council of Architectural Registration Boards (NCARB). Certification requires a professional architecture degree earned from a National Architectural Accrediting Board (NAAB)-accredited program, satisfactory completion of the Intern Development Program (IDP) training requirements, passing scores on the nine divisions of the Architect Registration Examination (ARE), application for and receipt of a license to practice from one of NCARB's member registration boards, and application for the NCARB Certificate. Continuing education requirements for registration renewal are set by the state(s) in which the architect is registered and practices.

Core Competencies and Skills Needed:
- Ability to visualize completed structures
- Competence in computer-aided design technology
- Knowledge of person-environment fit conceptual frameworks

Compensation: This varies by the type of practice and position within an architectural firm, the level of professional education and experience, and the geographical location of the practice.

Workplace(s): These include independent consultancies, sole proprietor practices, architectural firms, corporate architecture departments, and long-term care facilities.

Employment Outlook: Moderate—with excellent potential for expanding opportunities due to an increase in the number and variety of independent living communities, continuum of care residential communities and centers for elders, long-term care facilities (including demential care units) for frail and at-risk older adults, and free-standing hospice facilities.

Related Professional Organizations and Web Sites:
- The American Institute of Architects: www.aia.org
- American Institute of Architect Students: www.aias.org
- National Architectural Accrediting Board, Inc.: www.naab.org
- National Council of Architectural Registration Boards: www.ncarb.org

- The Association of Collegiate Schools of Architecture (ACSA): www. acsa-arch.org
- Society for the Advancement of Gerontological Environments (SAGE): www.sagefederation.org
- Environment and Gerontology Network (edra): www.edra.org
- Institute on Aging and Environment: www.uwm.edu/Dept/IAE

An Interview with
Andrew Lee Alden
Project Designer, Architecture Firm

What is your educational background in gerontology and other disciplines or professional fields? What formal credentials (e.g., completed degrees, certification) do you hold in these fields?

I have a Bachelor's of Science degree in Psychology and a Master's of Architecture degree. I am currently in the process of obtaining Architectural Registration through the State of Wisconsin.

Briefly describe your gerontology-related career path.

As an undergraduate psychology student, I was exposed to gerontological issues, but it wasn't until graduate school that I started to focus heavily on gerontology in my studies. While in graduate school at the University of Wisconsin at Milwaukee, I got involved with the Institute on Aging and Environment, which is located in the School of Architecture and Urban Planning. The Institute focuses on gerontological/ geriatric environments and consults on projects across the country. Through my involvement at the Institute and the mentoring of a faculty member, I gained an understanding of the impact environments can have on the lives and well-being of older adults. I was suddenly able to apply my psychology background to an architectural purpose. My master's thesis was a research study that examined the impact a new skilled nursing facility had on the residents, staff, and families.

How did you first become interested in your current professional position?

My formative years were heavily influenced by my aunts and uncles. My father was the youngest of a very large family, so I was surrounded by "elders" at every stage in my life. My uncle George, who was in his late 70s when we started to "hang-out" together, had a passion for preservation; he also was a successful machinist and businessman. He involved me in designing, building, and restoring everything from houses to a 19th century bank vault. My desire to create stayed strong in the years that followed and was not always connected with whatever "job" I currently held. After pursing paths in psychology, medicine, and business, it seemed I would never find the one profession to encompass all of my various areas of interest. I must admit that it was only upon my wife's suggestion for me to pursue a career in architecture that I began serious investigation of this possibility.

What are the most rewarding aspects of your career?

It's not just about having the privilege to materialize my imagination; it's about the impact that ideas can have. When I encounter someone who has been affected by my ideas, whether it's a hospice setting or an adult day services center, it's rewarding and humbling. The following comment from a family member of a hospice resident always lingers in my mind. "He was at peace. As soon as we arrived, he breathed a sigh of relief, as did we all. The place was great and it really made a difference to him and us." The environment can make a dramatic difference on the experience of the resident and his/her family.

What are the most challenging aspects of your career?

It can be challenging to achieve a design that meets all of my client's needs and is innovative. The truth is that no design is perfect or complete; I could work on one design for a lifetime and still not "finish it." The challenge is learning when to stop and reaching a point that balances the needs of my client, budget, and my own need for perfection.

Describe a typical workday in your current professional position.

Every day has the potential to be very different. Balancing numerous projects in different stages of design and construction often results in interesting "adventures" both outside and inside the office. If I am in the office, I spend the time answering questions from contractors, developing design ideas, reviewing marketing material, working on client presentations, or looking for design inspiration in books and magazines. If I am out of the office, I visit job sites or meet with existing or potential clients. I make sure to stay up to date on the latest research in my field and incorporate that information into my designs. I regularly read numerous journals and attend national conferences in an attempt to keep up with this constantly evolving field.

How do you balance career and other aspects of your life?

It takes constant effort to keep a balance, since architecture is not necessarily a 9 to 5 occupation. Given the limited amount of hours in the days, I make it a point to schedule and organize both my professional and personal activities. Deadlines are a fact of life in the architecture business; I have learned that an early start can help reach those goals, because it's easier to be productive when I can guarantee an hour or two of uninterrupted work. Architectural projects tend to be large multiple-month endeavors; I am not going to complete it in one day, even if I work late. The secret to completing a large project and enjoying the other aspects of my life is dividing up the tasks into manageable daily activities and accepting that tomorrow is another day to work on the design. Still, though, finding balance between my career and other aspects of my life is a work in progress.

What advice do you have for someone contemplating a career in gerontology? In a professional position similar to your current position?

The beauty of architecture is that your educational background and experience does not have to be solely architecture-related. As an example, my own background in psychology has enriched my interests in the architecture profession. Many universities around the country offer a Master's degree program in architecture to students with undergraduate degrees in other fields. Architecture with a gerontological specialty is a fast-growing field and offers many opportunities. My advice is to follow all of your passions, as diverse as they may seem. It is only when we figure out a way to combine all of the things we love in the world that we can truly find that "job" that becomes our passion. Architecture is my professional passion.

Art Therapist

Basic Description: Art therapy is used predominantly in mental health, human service, educational, medical, and social settings to help clients achieve positive outcomes, such as greater self-awareness and self-esteem, resolution of intra- and inter-personal conflicts, development of new social and coping skills, reduction of anxiety, improvement in how problems are handled, appropriate changes in reality orientation, and acquisition of helpful personal insights. Psychology and human development, especially adult development and aging, provide the theoretical foundation for art therapy. Art therapists draw on this interdisciplinary background for assessment and treatment models, tools, and strategies from cognitive, educational, psychodynamic, transpersonal, and other perspectives. They involve patients and clients in creative art processes (e.g., painting, drawing, creating fiber art, or pottery) to encourage self-expression through creation of their own artworks. They also observe their clients' reactions to already produced art objects (e.g., sculpture, pottery, paintings) as a means to understanding their individual developmental level, personality, interests, abilities, concerns, problems and conflicts, and potential for growth. The professional tasks of art therapists include selection of appropriate materials and interventions; determination of goals and objectives for clients to achieve maintenance of relevant case records; preparation of periodic reports; consultation with clients, family members, caregivers, and professional colleagues; participation in staff meetings and multidisciplinary healthcare teams; and involvement with professional organizations and conferences. In addition to their direct practice with patients, art therapists may serve as unit supervisors, agency administrators, and expert witnesses in court cases involving their clients.

Education and Experience Requirements: A minimum of a master's degree in art therapy is required for licensure and practice. Acceptance to a graduate degree program in this field requires a bachelor's degree from an accredited college/university, documentation of 15 semester hours in studio art and 12 semester hours in psychology prior to application, and the submission of a portfolio of original art.

Certification, Licensure, and Continuing Education Requirements:
The Art Therapy Credentials Board Inc. (ATCB) is the credentialing body. Attaining the Art Therapist Registered (ATR) designation requires documentation that the candidate has completed the proper master's degree and the required postgraduate experience. ATRs who pass the ATCB written examination are qualified as Board Certified (ATR-BC). Continuing education is required for recertification every 5 years.

Core Competencies and Skills Needed:
- Familiarity with and skill in the use of an array of art media
- Sensitivity to an array of older adult needs and interests
- Capacity for insight into the psychological processes of older adults
- Attentive listener
- Keen observer
- Emotional stability
- Patience
- Strong interpersonal skills; ability to develop rapport with older clients
- Ability to work effectively with a wide range of mental, emotional, physical, and social healthcare needs
- Ability to work effectively in a variety of settings
- Flexibility; ability to adapt
- Sense of humor

Compensation: This varies by one's education, experience, licensure, type of practice, nature of the practice setting, and the geographical location.

Workplace(s): These include hospitals and clinics (medical and psychiatric), hospice, wellness centers, social services agencies, outpatient mental health agencies and day treatment programs, educational programs and services, long-term care and assisted living facilities, senior centers and other community-based programs that serve elders, adult and intergenerational day care programs and centers, substance abuse and chemical dependency programs and agencies, rehabilitation and residential treatment centers, domestic violence and homeless shelters, community agencies and nonprofit organizations, correctional facilities, and independent private practices or consultancies.

Employment Outlook: Good—with an increasing potential for practice as the population grows older and as older persons become more comfortable with mental health therapies and human service interventions.

Related Professional Organizations and Web Sites:
- American Art Therapy Association, Inc. (AATA): www.arttherapy.org
- Art Therapy Credentials Board (ATCB): www.atcb.org
- National Coalition of Creative Arts Therapies Associations (NCCATA): www.nccata.org

Audiologist

Basic Description: Audiologists are experts in the nonmedical management of the auditory (hearing) and balance systems of the human body. Their work with clients is related to normal and impaired hearing, prevention of hearing loss, identification and assessment of hearing and balance problems, and rehabilitation of persons with hearing and balance disorders. Some audiologists also design hearing instruments and testing equipment; conduct research to add to the knowledge about normal hearing, hearing evaluation, and treatment of hearing and balance disorders; manage agencies, clinics, or private practices; or assist in the education of future audiology professionals through their work as professors or clinical supervisors and trainers. Audiologists in clinical practice frequently work with speech-language pathologists and medical specialists; some serve on interdisciplinary health care teams. Some audiologists also hold credentials and practice as speech-language pathologists (see Speech-Language Pathologist).

Education and Experience Requirements: A master's degree with an emphasis in audiology or a doctorate in audiology (AuD) is required. Undergraduate students may complete a bachelor's degree in communication sciences that includes audiology coursework, but a degree in audiology is not available at the undergraduate level. Gerontology coursework or a degree component is strongly recommended.

Certification, Licensure, and Continuing Education Requirements: For licensure, audiologists must meet the regulatory (licensure) standards in the state(s) where the practice occurs. For certification, individuals who hold a graduate degree in audiology are eligible for the Certificate of Clinical Competence in Audiology (CCC-A), which is issued by the Council for Clinical Certification in Audiology and Speech-Language Pathology (CFCC) of the American Speech-Language-Hearing Association (ASHA). Requirements include a graduate degree in audiology, 375 hours of supervised clinical experience, a 36 week postgraduate clinical fellowship, and a written examination.

Core Competencies and Skills Needed:
- Good listening skills
- Good oral and written communication skills, including:

- ability to effectively communicate diagnostic test results
- ability to relate to patients/clients and their caregivers/families about diagnosis and rehabilitation plans
- ability to explain technology developments and devices that assist patients/clients with hearing loss
- ability to propose and interpret treatment so that is easily understood by clients and other professionals
- Objective approach to problems
- Patience
- Compassion
- Capable of providing appropriate support for clients/patients and their caregivers/families

Compensation: This varies according to one's educational background, certification, experience, nature of practice, type of practice setting, and geographical location.

Workplace(s): These include hospitals, medical centers, rehabilitation centers, residential health facilities, community clinics, private practice offices, long-term care facilities, community hearing and speech centers, physicians' offices, research laboratories, and consultancies with local, state, and government agencies and organizations that serve elders.

Employment Outlook: Excellent—with faster than average growth expected through 2012 due to an increased demand for audiologists in private practice to provide direct services to individuals and to the increased use of contract services by hospitals, medical centers, and long-term nursing care facilities.

Related Professional Organizations and Web Sites:
- American Speech-Language-Hearing Association (ASHA): www.asha.org

An Interview with
Kathleen M. Sawhill,
Audiologist

What is your educational background in gerontology and other disciplines or professional fields? What formal credentials (e.g., completed degrees, certification) do you hold in these fields?

I earned a bachelor's degree (BS) in communication disorders, with minors in human development and gerontology in 2002. I graduated with my Doctorate of Audiology (AuD) in 2006. Following completion of my AuD degree, I obtained my license in audiology from the state of Michigan and also became certified by the American Speech-Language-Hearing Association (ASHA).

Briefly describe your gerontology-related career path.

My formal education in gerontology affirmed my desire to work with older adults. In completing this portion of my degree, I was able to work with and research the dynamics of the aging population. Specific educational opportunities, such as volunteering for the Michigan Senior Olympics, studying the welfare state in Sweden, and completing a project on sister relationships in late life, furthered my interest and knowledge regarding the elderly population. This interest grew into a desire to improve the quality of life for elders and encouraged me to pursue a career in which I would be able to do so. I have been working at my current place of employment, a medical center, for approximately two years now. The first year was in fulfillment of an externship for my doctoral degree. Upon graduation, I remained on staff as a member of the team of audiologists.

How did you first become interested in your current professional position?

I have always wanted to pursue a career that would allow me to work with others. I originally set out on a career path towards elementary education, but soon learned that this was not my passion. I longed for a career that would enable me to work with a variety of ages on an individual basis. Early in my undergraduate coursework, I decided to explore my options and took an introductory course in speech and hearing disorders. I found the assessment and treatment of hearing and balance disorders to be very interesting. The profession of audiology would enable me to work primarily with elders and to assist them with their communicative needs. I soon signed a major in communication disorders and never looked back.

What are the most rewarding aspects of your career?

By far, the most rewarding aspect of my career is my ability to make a difference in the quality of people's lives. Living with hearing loss not only impairs the ability to communicate effectively, but also leads to social isolation and depression. To be able to provide a means of giving people part of their life back is something that I feel very fortunate to do.

What are the most challenging aspects of your career?

One of the most challenging aspects of my career is in counseling individuals regarding the limitations of hearing aids. Oftentimes, patients expect that hearing aids will return their hearing back to normal. Hearing aid technology has improved immensely in recent years and can provide a significant improvement in hearing for those with hearing loss, however, a hearing aid is still an "aid." Nothing can replace the hearing that has been lost. Individuals who have made the decision to work with an audiologist and wish to pursue amplification can typically expect to receive significant auditory benefit; however, individuals with hearing loss still need to be consciously aware of their hearing loss, the limitations of the hearing aids, and must be committed to learning to hear differently.

Describe a typical workday in your current professional position.

Most days I can be found working onsite at the medical center. I am currently one of six audiologists at this facility. Each day is different from the next, but on any given day I typically perform hearing assessments, discuss appropriate amplification options with those with hearing impairment, and fit and program hearing aids. For those patients suffering from dizziness or imbalance difficulties, my current position enables me to perform vestibular testing, which is a test to evaluate the function of the balance system. I also perform auditory evoked potential testing, which is utilized to determine the presence of hearing loss in very young children, or may also be used to rule out the presence of a retro cochlear lesion.

How do you balance career and other aspects of your life?

I find a great deal of satisfaction in assisting those with hearing loss, however, as with many careers, it includes a fair amount of stress and frustration. I'm new to this career and am still learning to balance my personal life and my career.

What advice do you have for someone contemplating a career in gerontology? In a professional position similar to your current position?

I think that careers in gerontology hold a great deal of promise for the future. Due to the rapid growth of the elderly population and the improvements in hearing aid technology, the field of audiology is expected to flourish in coming years. In fact, audiologist recently was ranked as one of the top career choices by a major news magazine. I would encourage those considering a career in audiology to, first and foremost, spend considerable time with a group of elders. Volunteering offers endless possibilities for working with older people and may help to affirm a possible career choice. For those who do find great satisfaction and enjoyment in working with elders, who like working in a small clinic setting and are interested in the technological advancements of the medical industry, I strongly encourage them to consider a career in audiology.

Career and Employment Counselor

Basic Description: Career and employment counselors (sometimes titled "career counselors" or "employment counselors") assist individuals who are seeking employment or assistance with employment or career reentry, career development and transition, and work-to-retirement transitions. Although their clients traditionally have been adolescents and young or middle-aged adults, they now find older adults among their clientele. Using the tools of the professional field in which they were trained, career and employment counselors assess their clients' work-related skills, abilities, and interests and then assist their clients with work-related training or retraining, career development, job search, and job entry. While they use similar processes with clients of all ages, career and employment counselors who specialize in working with older adults must be sensitive to the factors that shape an older person's need or desire for employment, regardless of whether that need is related to remaining in the workforce rather than retiring, entering the workforce for the first time in later life, reentering the workforce after an extended time out of it, making a work-to-retirement transition, or returning to full- or part-time employment after an earlier retirement. Some career/employment professionals (such as personnel administrators or human resources managers) hold positions in corporate settings where they are responsible for recruitment, hiring, and supervision of older workers, oversight of laws and regulations specific to older workers, and work-to-retirement transitions. Others work with government needs-based employment programs (such as Foster Grandparents Program, Senior Companion Program, and Green Thumb) for older persons.

Education and Experience Requirements: A bachelor's degree or higher in counseling and guidance, personnel administration, adult education, or closely related field is required. A master's degree is preferred or required by some professions and employing agencies. Gerontology coursework or a degree component is strongly recommended.

Certification, Licensure, and Continuing Education Requirements: Career and employment counselors must meet the licensure or certification requirements in the state where the professional practice occurs. Continuing education or post-degree supervised clinical training may be required for some professions or employing agencies.

Core Competencies and Skills Needed:
- Good understanding of the factors related to older adults' needs and/or desires to work
- Good working knowledge of laws and regulations related to older workers and age discrimination in the workplace
- Respect for the talents and skills of older adults in regard to career
- Ability to establish trusting, open, and useful relationships with older clients
- Commitment to a client-centered practice
- Ability to facilitate decisionmaking and goalsetting
- Computer literacy on relevant software and databases
- Excellent verbal and written communication skills
- Attentive listening skills
- Ability to maintain confidentiality
- Good organizational skills

Compensation: This varies by one's education, experience, type of position, level of responsibility, and the nature of employment setting.

Workplace(s): These include community-based career counseling centers and adult education programs; corporate human resources departments; community college, college and university career counseling centers; centers and agencies that serve elders; and Senior Community Service Employment Programs (SCSEP).

Employment Outlook: Limited at current time—but is nevertheless promising due to an increase in the size of the older adult population and an increase in the number of older adults who are interested in employment and career development opportunities.

Related Professional Organizations and Web Sites:
- American Counseling Association (ACA): www.counseling.org
- National Employment Counseling Association (NECA): www.employmentcounseling.org/neca.html
- Maturity Works Alliance (MWA), National Council on Aging (NCOA): www.ncoa.org
- National Older Worker Career Center (NOWCC): www.nowcc.org
- Senior Community Service Employment Program (SCSEP): www.doleta.gov/seniors
- National Career Development Association (NCDA): www.ncda.org
- National Board for Certified Counselors (NBCC): www.nbcc.org
- Center on Adult, Career, & Vocational Education (ACVE), Ohio State University: www.cete.org/acve

Certified Aging-in-Place Specialist (CAPs)

Basic Description: Certified Aging-in-Place Specialists (CAPS) assist people of all ages to continue living independently, safely, and comfortably in their own homes, regardless of their income, health status, and functional level. Professionals with the CAPS designation include building contractors and remodelers, architects, interior designers, reverse mortgage specialists, environmental gerontologists, certified senior advisors, occupational and physical therapists, and aging consultants.

Education and Experience Requirements: Educational requirements include completion of an appropriate degree or training program for the base profession, completion of the CAPS educational program (courses on working with and marketing to older adults, home modifications, and introduction to business management); and submission of a graduation application to the National Association of Home Builders University of Housing (NAHB).

Certification, Licensure, and Continuing Education Requirements: Additional continuing education and/or participation in community service is required every three years.

Core Competencies and Skills Needed:
- Understand the meaning of *home* to each specific client
- Know and stay updated on relevant building codes, standards, and materials
- Practice excellent interpersonal communication skills
- Recognize impact of physical, mental, and social health on housing needs of aging persons
- Meet requirements for practice in their primary profession

Compensation: This varies by type of career position, nature of the employment setting, educational background, experience, part- or full-time position, and geographical location.

Workplace(s): These include building and remodeling contract firms, banks, interior design studios, private consulting firms, agencies that serve elders, and community and human service agencies.

Employment Outlook: High—but varies by type of profession; actual demand is not yet established for professionals with this relatively new certification.

Related Professional Organizations and Web Sites:
- National Association of Home Builders (NAHB): www.nahb.org
- National Aging in Place Council (NAIPC): www.naipc.org

Certified Geriatric Pharmacist (CPG)

Basic Description: Certified Geriatric Pharmacists (CPGs; see Consultant Pharmacist or Senior Care Pharmacist) have earned the CGP designation by meeting three criteria: they hold a valid pharmacy license, they have 2 or more years of experience in pharmacy practice, and they have successfully passed the 150-item, multiple-choice certification examination in geriatric pharmacy that tests candidates' knowledge in three areas of practice: patient-specific activities (34% of exam), disease-specific activities (56% of exam), and quality improvement/utilization management activities (10% of exam).

Education and Experience Requirements: CGPs require a Doctor of Pharmacy (PharmD) degree from an American Council for Pharmacy Education (APCE)-accredited school of pharmacy.

Certification, Licensure, and Continuing Education Requirements: Recertification is required every 5 years and can be obtained by either passing a multiple-choice 150-question examination administered by the Commission for Certification of Geriatric Pharmacists (CCGP) or by earning 75 continuing education hours through the recently approved American Society of Consultant Pharmacists (ASCP) professional development program for CGPs.

Core Competencies and Skills Needed:
- Competence in patient-centered practice with older adults and geriatric patients
- Research-based understanding of the aging process and factors that affect the physical, mental, and social health of elders
- Excellent understanding of geriatric pharmacotherapy specific to disease-specific conditions of patients

- Excellent communication and interpersonal skills
- Ability to educate patients about the proper and safe use of medications and other pharmacy-related therapies
- Commitment to prevention of misuse and abuse of medications and over-the-counter drugs
- Commitment to ethical practice with elderly and frail clients

Compensation: This varies by the type of practice, education, experience, place of employment, level of position held, and geographical location.

Workplace(s): These include community-based pharmacies, hospital and medical care center pharmacies, nursing facilities, subacute care and assisted living facilities, psychiatric hospitals, hospice programs, and home and community-based care organizations.

Employment Outlook: Excellent.

Related Professional Organizations and Web Sites:
- American Society of Consultant Pharmacists (ASCP): www.ascp.com
- Commission for Certification in Geriatric Pharmacy (CCGP): www.ccgp.org
- American Council for Pharmacy Education (ACPE): www.acpe-accredit.org

---

Consultant or Senior Care Pharmacist

Basic Description: Consultant pharmacists and senior care pharmacists practice patient-centered pharmacotherapy that recognizes the complexity of inter-relationships between disease states, injury statuses, nutrition, medications, and other variables. They commonly work as a member of a health care team. In working with and on behalf of patients, they provide information and recommendations to subscribers and caregivers; review patients' drug regimens; educate and counsel patients about appropriate and safe use of medications; present in-service educational and training programs for facility staff members, family caregivers, and the lay public; oversee medication distribution services in the facility; provide related services such as pain management counseling, pharmacokinetic dosing services, intravenous therapy, nutrition assessment and support, and durable medical equipment; and identify, resolve, and prevent medication-related problems.

Education and Experience Requirements: This position requires a minimum of a BS or MS in pharmacy. A PharmD degree is strongly recommended and is required by some employing agencies and consultation settings.

Certification, Licensure, and Continuing Education Requirements: Consultant pharmacists and senior care pharmacists must have a valid pharmacy license in the state(s) where the practice occurs; stay current with changing laws and regulations about medications and the settings in which they practice; and maintain or improve their level of knowledge and practice competence through post-graduate residencies, experiential traineeships, and continuing pharmaceutical education.

Core Competencies and Skills Needed:
- Knowledge and skills in geriatric pharmacotherapy and the unique medication-related needs of elders and long-term care residents
- Expertise in long-term care settings for frail and at-risk elders
- Patient-centered advocacy skills
- Current knowledge of state and federal pharmacy laws applicable to practice setting(s)
- Ability to work collaboratively as a member of an interdisciplinary health care team
- Good organizational skills
- Good written and oral communication skills

Compensation: This varies by education, experience, practice setting, type and level of professional position, and geographical location.

Workplace(s): These include hospitals, medical centers and clinics, long-term care and nursing facilities, subacute care and assisted living facilities, psychiatric hospitals, hospice, and home- and community-based care programs.

Employment Outlook: Excellent.

Related Professional Organizations and Web Sites:
- American Society of Consultant Pharmacists (ASCP): www.ascp.com (profiles of several consulting pharmacists and senior care pharmacists are available at this Web site)
- American Pharmacists Association (APhA): www.aphanet.org
- Accreditation Council for Pharmacy Education (ACPE): www.acpe-accredit.org
- National Association of Boards of Pharmacy (NABP): www.nabp.net

Certified Senior Advisor (CSA)

Basic Description: Certified Senior Advisors (CSAs) are professionals from a wide variety of fields (e.g., accounting, law, business, clergy, medicine, nursing, pharmacy, financial planning, funeral services, geriatric care, home health care, insurance, realty, mortgage lending, housing, social work) who have earned the CSA designation to add to the credentials they hold in their primary professional field(s). The CSA education program integrates the social, health, and financial aspects of aging to help professionals focus on people rather than products. By having a better understanding of their aging and elderly clients, CSAs fit their products and services to the needs and interests of the clients.

Education and Experience Requirements: Applicants for CSA training must hold valid credentials in their field(s) of practice, complete CSA program requirements, and pass the CSA Designation Exam.

Certification, Licensure, and Continuing Education Requirements: CSAs must complete an annual renewal statement, pay annual renewal dues, and complete 128 CSA continuing education credits every 3 years.

Core Competencies and Skills Needed:
- Good written and communication skills
- Attentive listener
- Good interpersonal skills
- Good organizational skills
- Commitment to client-centered practice
- Ethical conduct of business/professional practice
- Competencies specific to primary professional field(s) and practice standards

Compensation: This varies by the type of professional practice, educational background, experience, and geographical location.

Workplace(s): This varies by the type of professional practice.

Employment Outlook: Moderate to high—depending on the type of professional practice.

Related Professional Organizations and Web Sites:
- Society of Certified Senior Advisors: www.society-csa.com

Certified Social Worker in Gerontology (CSW-G) Certified Advanced Social Worker in Gerontology (CASW-G) Certified Advanced Clinical Social Worker in Gerontology (CACSW-G)

Basic Description: According to the National Association of Social Workers (NASW) and the Council on Social Work Education (CSWE), a "professional social worker" is a graduate of a CWSE-accredited social work program at the bachelor's (BSW), master's (MSW), or doctoral (DSW) level. Social workers with BSW and MSW degrees assess the needs of older adults, their families, caregivers, and social support network; provide information about and referrals to programs and services to meet these needs; and evaluate the outcomes of the services provided. At times the social workers provide the services needed (such as care and case management, counseling, or education). The primary goals of social workers in direct practice with older adults include maintaining independence and self-determination, assuring adequate financial resources through income assistance programs, promoting and maintaining the well-being of elders and their families, and improving the quality of life for their elderly clients. While the majority of social workers are in direct practice roles and positions, some work on behalf of elders through advocacy, policy development, and policy enactment. Recently, NASW added three levels of certification for gerontological social workers (see *Certification* below). Another initiative to improve social work practice with elders is the Masters Advanced Curriculum (MAC) Project, which is designed to infuse gerontological competencies into three MSW specialty practice areas: mental health, substance abuse, and health.

Education and Experience Requirements: A minimum of a BSW degree is required for entry-level direct service positions in human service agencies. A MSW degree is preferred for many entry-level positions and is required for clinical social work and most positions involving supervisory, administrative, planning and policy responsibilities. A Doctor of Social Work (DSW) degree is required for most academic teaching and research positions.

Certification, Licensure, and Continuing Education Requirements: Licensure is required in the state where the professional practice occurs, and may require passing an examination. A specified amount of continuing education and full-time or equivalent practice are required for license renewal. The NASW now has three levels of certification for gerontological social workers: Certified Social Worker in Gerontology (CSW-G), Certified Advanced Social Worker in Gerontology (CASW-G), and Certified Advanced Clinical Social Worker in Gerontology (CACSW-G). Certification is earned through a combination of a BSW or MSW degree, years or equivalent hours of experience working with older adults under social work supervision, continuing education, exam-based licensure, and adherence to NASW codes of ethics and standards.

Core Competencies and Skills Needed:
- Commitment to culturally sensitive professional practice
- Good communication (oral, written, and listening) skills
- Good interpersonal skills
- Patience, persistence, perseverance
- Good organizational skills
- Good working knowledge of programs, services, and facilities for older adults
- Good working knowledge of regulations and legislation related to provision of services to older adults

Compensation: This varies by education, experience, licensure, certification level, type of position, nature of employment setting, and geographical location.

Workplace(s): These include adult day care centers and programs, public social service agencies, adult protective services, county units (e.g., commissions, departments, bureaus) on aging, Area Agencies on Aging (AAAs), information and referral agencies, alcohol and substance abuse services, hospitals and medical centers, outpatient primary care settings (e.g., group medical and dental practices), assisted living facilities, long-term care facilities, rehabilitation centers, hospice and bereavement service programs, respite programs, elder abuse & neglect centers/programs, faith-based organizations, home health care, family services agencies, life care communities, mental health agencies/centers, ombudsperson and advocacy programs, senior centers, senior housing centers and retirement communities, research centers/institutes, veterans' services, corporate eldercare programs and firms, courts and legal/paralegal services and firms, managed care organizations, Social Security Administration offices (Medicare, Medicaid, and SSI), federal and state offices and programs for older adults (e.g., Senior Health Counseling and Assistance Program, Senior Companion, Foster Grandparent, and RSVP), banks and investment firms, and insurance companies.

Employment Outlook: Excellent—demand currently exceeds supply, especially at MSW and DSW degree levels.

Related Professional Organizations and Web Sites:
* National Association of Social Workers (NASW): www.socialworkers.org
* Council on Social Work Education (CSWE): www.cswe.org
* CSWE Gero-Ed Center: http://depts.washington.edu/geroctr

Clinical Geropsychologist

Basic Description: Clinical Geropsychology was first recognized as a Proficiency by the American Psychological Association (APA) in 1998 (recognition renewal will be required in 2008). Clinical geropsychologists work with older adults, their families and/or caregivers to maintain well-being both of the older adult and within the family system; stabilize or overcome mental, emotional, and behavioral problems; and optimize the potential and quality of life for the elders they treat. They assess, consult, and provide intervention services related to psychological adaptations in later life, psychopathology, behavioral problems, problems in daily living, medical and legal decision-making capacity, independent living arrangements, behavioral competencies, and sociocultural/socioeconomic factors that influence the experience and expression of psychological problems. Clinical geropsychologists use several types of intervention that are unique to work with an older clientele; these interventions include reminiscence, memory enhancement, life review, grief work, and other expressive therapies. They also offer psychoeducational programs and support groups for family caregivers. Some geropsychologists serve as interdisciplinary health care team members that do comprehensive geriatric assessments.

Education and Experience Requirements: A Doctor of Philosophy (PhD) or Doctor of Psychology (PsyD) in clinical psychology is required. Coursework or a degree component/emphasis in gerontology is strongly recommended. Postdoctoral fellowships are encouraged, especially for those with research interests.

Certification, Licensure, and Continuing Education Requirements: Clinical geropsychologists must meet licensure requirements in the state where the professional practice occurs. Continuing education may be required for license renewal or by an employing agency.

Core Competencies and Skills Needed:
- Competencies and skills are outlined for the following aspects of geropsychology practice: attitudes; general knowledge about adult development, aging, and older adults; clinical issues; assessment; intervention, consultation, and other service provision; education (see further information on APA Web site)
- Good listener
- Good interpersonal skills
- Good communication skills
- Patience and calm demeanor

Compensation: This varies by education, experience, specific type of practice, and the nature of the employing agency, organization, or facility.

Workplace(s): These include medical centers, in-patient medical or psychiatric hospital units, geropsychology clinics and institutes, long-term care facilities, health care management corporations, community mental health agencies, community substance abuse programs and agencies, organizations specific to mental health disorders (e.g., Alzheimer's disease, depression, Parkinson's disease), independent or group private practice, outpatient settings, day care programs, and home care agencies.

Employment Outlook: Good—with the potential for increased demand due to rapid growth in the elderly population over the next few decades.

Related Professional Organizations and Web Sites:
- American Psychological Association (APA): www.apa.org
- Formal Interest Group on Mental Health Practice and Aging, Gerontological Society of America (GSA): www.geron.org
- Informal Interest Group on Emotion and Aging, Gerontological Society of America (GSA): www.geron.org
- Mental Health and Aging Network (MHAN), American Society on Aging (ASA): www.asaging.org

Communications Director, National Membership Organization

Basic Description: Communications Directors are responsible for developing and carrying out all communication efforts in support of an organization's mission and goals, which often are diverse in nature. Responsibilities include the preparation of all print, electronic, and other media communications (such as press releases, letters to the editor, opinion editorials, brochures, booklets, fact sheets, and other publications). Communications directors also monitor the press (print and electronic), develop the organization's relations with the media and the public, create press opportunities for the organization, and lead promotion for the organization's annual conference, policy briefings, and other events. It is also now more common for communications directors to provide oversight for or development of the organization's Web site and its content.

Education and Experience Requirements: A bachelor's degree or higher and 5 or more years of experience in communications or a closely related field (such as public relations or journalism) is the minimum. Experience in Web site management and graphical print presentations is preferred.

Core Competencies and Skills Needed:
- Excellent writing and editing skills
- Demonstrated success with media (such as published or aired opinion editorials)
- Excellent verbal and written communication skills
- Excellent interpersonal skills
- Ability to work in a fast-paced office
- Ability to juggle multiple priorities and multitask
- Good computer skills related to word processing and other relevant software
- Ability to work effectively in a small office space
- Ability to follow directions and take instruction, as needed

- Ability to work in a team and switch hats, as needed, between being the team leader or a team member

Compensation: This varies by education, experience, level of position, specified job responsibilities, the nature of the employing organization, and geographical location.

Workplace(s): These include organization headquarters, which are usually located in a larger city (e.g., San Francisco, Chicago, Washington, DC).

Employment Outlook: Good.

Related Professional Organizations and Web Sites:

- Web sites of national member organizations and associations

---

Continuing Care Retirement Community Administrator Long-Term Care Facility Administrator

Basic Description: Administrators of residential care facilities, such as continuing care retirement communities and long-term care facilities, direct and/or oversee all operational aspects of the facility, including personnel and labor assessment, training, human resources, and evaluation; labor union relationships; regulatory, licensure, and organizational/facility policies and procedures compliance; property assessment and management; supervision of resident care; food services; risk management; physical plant maintenance; facility/community operating systems; marketing and public relations; budget and revenue; and reporting and liaison functions with community or facility boards and corporate leadership. Administrators are also responsible for long-term strategic planning and initiatives.

Education and Experience Requirements: A bachelor's degree or higher is the minimum requirement; a master's degree in healthcare administration, long-term care administration, hospital administration, or a closely related field is preferred. Also, a minimum of 3–5 years of health care administrative experience is required.

Certification, Licensure, and Continuing Education Requirements: Administrators must meet nursing home administrator licensure in the state where the professional practice occurs. Continuing education may be required for licensure renewal, job tenure, and/or advancement.

Core Competencies and Skills Needed:
- Understanding of long-term care market and operations
- Strong financial acumen
- Sensitive to labor issues
- Knowledge of state and federal regulations specific to type of facility
- Genuine passion for improving quality of life for older adults
- Commitment to client-centered care
- Demonstrated leadership capacity and ability
- Strong team orientation
- Demonstrated credibility, discipline, follow-through, and consistency
- Enthusiasm and energy
- Self-motivated
- Excellent oral and written communication skills
- Attentive listener
- Excellent interpersonal skills

Compensation: This varies by education, experience, the nature of the employment setting, the level of responsibility within the total organization, and geographical location.

Workplace(s): These include assisted living and long-term care facilities, continuum of care communities, long-term care corporations, and dementia care units.

Employment Outlook: Good—may be influenced by the increasing focus on aging in place in independent living situations, growth of the in-home care industry, and the legislative focus on deinstitutionalization.

Related Professional Organizations and Web Sites:
- American Association of Homes and Services for the Aging (AAHSA): www. aahsa.org
- Healthcare and Aging Network (HAN), American Society on Aging (ASA): www.asaging.org
- Mental Health and Aging Network (MHAN), American Society on Aging (ASA): www.asaging.org
- Formal Interest Group on Assisted Living, Gerontological Society of America (GSA): www.geron.org

An Interview with David J. Mancuso, Administrator, Continuing Care Retirement Community

What is your educational background in gerontology and other disciplines or professional fields? What formal credentials (e.g., completed degrees, certification) do you hold in these fields?

I have a Bachelor of Arts degree with a double major in political science and history. I also completed an undergraduate certificate program in gerontology. I also have a Master of Gerontological Studies degree. I am also a Licensed Nursing Home Administrator (LNHA) in the state of Ohio.

Briefly describe your gerontology-related career path.

As an undergraduate student, I completed a three-month internship with a community senior center. My duties consisted of fitness and activity related programming with local elders. During the brief time between my undergraduate and graduate level coursework, I worked as a summer employee for a senior center. My job focused on one-on-one activities for elders living independently in their apartments. As a graduate student, I completed a state of Ohio-approved 14-week Administrator-in-Training (AIT) program at a continuing care retirement community. Following my graduate level coursework, I was hired as the assistant administrator for a continuing care retirement community. A year later, I became the administrator.

How did you first become interested in your current professional position?

I was encouraged by one of my graduate school professors to pursue a position in long-term care administration.

What are the most rewarding aspects of your career?

I like working for a community-supported, nonprofit retirement community, with dedicated staff members who share the common goal of quality care and outstanding services, and for an employer that believes in me and recognizes my efforts. I enjoy building relationships and friendships with residents, family members, coworkers, community members, and community leaders. I like to make decisions that have positive outcomes on the lives of current and future residents. I enjoy working with donors to fundraise for an organization that I truly believe makes a positive difference.

What are the most challenging aspects of your career?

My greatest challenges are working through government regulations and reimbursement for services, anything related to red tape, and fitting in all of the daily demands of the job during the course of the day.

Describe a typical workday in your current professional position.

Every day is very unique. It begins in my office with a check of voicemail and e-mail. I then meet with key staff members for a brief update meeting. After that, the day becomes quite unpredictable. It may involve short- or long-range planning meetings or individual meetings with staff members, residents, family members, or donors. I may be involved with the interviewing, coaching, or disciplining of employees on any given day. There is always a daily occupancy and expense review. I spend time each day approving retirement community-related bills. Also, I am involved often with policy revisions and updates.

How do you balance career and other aspects of your life?

I don't balance my career and other aspects of my life very well. It seems like there is always something to do at work or a work-related event to attend. Thankfully, I love my job and I have a very supportive and understanding network at home.

What advice do you have for someone contemplating a career in gerontology? In a professional position similar to your current position?

The field of gerontology is an excellent career choice. It can be both stressful and rewarding. Someone considering a career similar to mine should have some background in business, marketing, management, and/or administration, in addition to their gerontological background, in order to be successful. Long-term care is not a nine-to-five job. We are open twenty-four hours every day. This field is not for everyone. Volunteering and internships are great ways to find out if this field is for you. I would recommend for everyone entering this field to be open-minded, flexible, thoughtful, and respectful of others. Always hire the best person available for open positions. If a star candidate comes along for an opening, find a way to make that person a part of your organization. Don't ever fear someone that you think might be smarter or more ambitious than you. Outstanding employees always make your organization better.

Cooperative Extension Service Specialist in Gerontology

Basic Description: The Extension Specialist in Gerontology provides state-wide leadership for the development, implementation, and evaluation of Cooperative Extension Service adult and youth programming in gerontology. Extension specialists design, conduct, and oversee a comprehensive applied research program plan (including research to evaluate program designs). They develop and present train-the-trainer in-service programs for county-based extension agents and prepare gerontology-specific or related materials for use with extension educational programs and by the lay public. Specialists also must maintain a collaborative working relationship with campus-based administrators and faculty members in relevant academic colleges, schools and departments; establish and maintain a cooperative working relationship with state, county, and community agencies and organizations that are related to the extension gerontology programs and research agenda; supervise and advise assigned graduate students; and report research and program results to the cooperative extension system, stakeholders, funding agencies, and key constituents through presentations for professional organizations and refereed publications. The tenure-track appointment, with academic rank at the assistant or associate professor level, is typically 75% cooperative extension and 25% research. Some appointments may hold the expectation for the specialist to teach credit-based courses for undergraduate or graduate students in gerontology or a related field.

Education and Experience Requirements: This position requires a PhD in gerontology, human development: adult development & aging, family studies/ family science, or a closely related field.

Certification, Licensure, and Continuing Education Requirements: None are required, however, specialists are expected to stay current on relevant research in gerontology, family studies, adult development and aging, and related fields. Active participation in appropriate national, regional, and state professional organizations is expected. Cooperative extension service specialists must meet tenure-track requirements for faculty appointment.

Core Competencies and Skills Needed:
- Commitment to an interdisciplinary approach to gerontology, individual/ family development, and consumer sciences
- Ability to conduct and interpret research and technical information in gerontology for the public
- Demonstrated proficiency in written and oral communication and presentation skills for diverse audiences
- Experience with extension and/or outreach program development, delivery, applied research, and publication
- Ability to work cooperatively with state agencies, the academic community, extension professionals, and the public
- Ability to prepare grant applications/proposals and administer grants and contracts
- Experience in planning, implementing, and evaluating nonformal gerontology programs
- Prior cooperative extension and teaching experience

Compensation: This varies according to the qualifications and experience of the applicant and may vary by state.

Workplace(s): Extension specialists are usually based on the campus of a state's land grant university. The position, however, requires extensive travel throughout the state.

Employment Outlook: Good— but is limited to one specialist per state.

Related Professional Organizations and Web Sites:
- National Council on Family Relations (NCFR): www.ncfr.org
- American Society on Aging (ASA): www.asaging.org
- Gerontological Society of America (GSA): www.geron.org

County Commission on Aging (COA) Director

Basic Description: A County Commission on Aging (COA) is a county-level governmental unit that is charged with providing Older Americans Act programs and services to persons who are 60 years of age and older. Although "county commission" is the commonly used term, some county units are titled differently (such as county department or bureau of aging) and some are multicounty units (such as a tri-county commission on aging). Regardless of the name of the unit, the directors of units are responsible for the overall administration of the agency. They prepare and administer grants related to aging services and programs; develop and oversee the commission's budget; oversee the recruitment, hiring, supervision, evaluation, and discipline of commission employees; serve as the primary liaison to the Area Agency on Aging and the state office on aging; and serve as the primary representative for the agency on county and state governing boards and committees. Additional responsibilities vary from one commission to another and may include working to establish and maintain a county-wide senior services millage or other local fundraising efforts, editing an agency newsletter, and other tasks related to meeting the needs of the agency's clients.

Education and Experience Requirements: A master's degree in public administration, social work, gerontology, or a closely related human service field is required. Coursework or degree components in gerontology, community organization and leadership, and/or public administration is recommended. A minimum of 3-5 years of administrative leadership experience in human service field or an aging network agency is required.

Certification, Licensure, and Continuing Education Requirements: None are required, but staying current is vital and can be obtained through either formal or informal continuing education.

Core Competencies and Skills Needed:
- Ability to work with and relate to older adults, their needs and concerns
- Ability to work with clients from diverse backgrounds
- Good working knowledge of the formal aging network
- Good working knowledge of regulations related to the commission's programs and services
- Ability to supervise others, including staff, volunteers, and clients
- Working knowledge of committee and board structures, functions, and processes
- Good written and oral communication skills
- Public speaking skills
- Grant writing skills
- Good financial management skills
- Good organizational skills

Compensation: This varies according to one's educational background, amount of field service and/or administrative experience, and the geographical location.

Workplace(s): These include county or multicounty units on aging, which are usually located in the largest city within the county(ies) served.

Employment Outlook: Good—but may be limited by the longevity of some COA directors (especially in more rural counties). Job prospects are also dependent on continued federal, state, and county funding for COAs.

Related Professional Organizations and Web Sites:
*   State organization for directors of services to the aging

An Interview with
Craig Zeese, County
Commission on Aging Director

What is your educational background in gerontology and other disciplines or professional fields? What formal credentials (e.g., completed degrees, certification) do you hold in these fields?

I have a Bachelor's of Social Work (BSW) degree, with minors in gerontology and psychology.

Briefly describe your gerontology-related career path.

I worked as a social worker for a county council on aging for three years, then relocated and worked as a social worker for another county commission on aging three more years. I was then promoted to Director of that county commission on aging and have been in this position for the past 20 years.

How did you first become interested in your current professional position?

My first volunteer experience with older persons was during my high school days when I visited residents in nursing homes as part of a service club's project. I had no family contact with elders (all of my grandparents were deceased before I was born), but this high school experience and completing volunteer work with older adults during my college career confirmed that working with older people in some capacity was what I wanted to do with my life.

What are the most rewarding aspects of your career?

Knowing that because of my leadership, older people are being helped every day in some way by a dedicated staff and through our direct in-home services is very fulfilling. Hearing comments from our clients and their families as to how helpful our agency is to them makes the job all worthwhile. Knowing that we are able to make a difference in a person's life and help keep them independent and in their own home is very rewarding. As a past social worker, having daily contact with elders and their families, making arrangements for services for them, and knowing that their quality of life was better because of my actions and the services being arranged was extremely rewarding.

What are the most challenging aspects of your career?

One of most challenging aspects is seeing how politics play a factor in funding and regulations of services and trying to convey the importance of these services and their impact to our elected representatives who really do decide how funding is to be distributed. Then, trying to fairly distribute available funds for services within the agency to make the most positive impact for our elderly clients is a challenge. Exploring and developing new resources (both formal and informal) that allow for additional programs is both exciting and challenging. Keeping peace within the staff can be difficult at times, because they are all passionate about their specific programs and they also want to help the clients they serve in the best way they can. Conveying to others about how important older adult services are and how they impact not only the elders, but also their families and the community in general, is another challenge that is crucial when I'm working to promote the need for a "senior millage" to be voted upon by the residents of the county.

Describe a typical workday in your current professional position.

There isn't a typical work day. In the course of a week, however, I usually spend some time on either preparing and writing of a grant, or at least working with existing grants and the regulations associated with them; preparing and working with the agency budget and other financial matters; attending work groups, committees, boards, and community activities where representation of older adults and/or the commission on aging is needed and expected; and dealing with personnel issues, such as unplanned illnesses, and trying to coordinate activities so that our services to clients are not disrupted. Work is completed weekly on articles submitted to newspapers and preparing/giving presentations in the community. I frequently meet with funding providers to work on issues at hand or with county administrators who are working on a multitude of policies that impact county government. Every day, though, there seems to be unexpected problems that arise. It could be problems due to weather when volunteers are delivering home-delivered meals. It could be a volunteer becoming lost when taking someone to an appointment. It could be an in-home service worker finding that a client has fallen and immediate medical action is necessary. It could be a mechanical problem at one of the senior centers and action is required to see that programs are not cancelled, or it could be a local food pantry calling to say that they have an overabundance of perishable food and they would like us to get it out to our elderly clients before it spoils. It is the unexpected situations needing immediate attention that cause the greatest stress.

How do you balance career and other aspects of your life?

It is extremely important to balance my family life and career. First, it is okay to say "no" to some projects. Next, I do believe it is important to be active with other community organizations. Socially, I am quite active with our local community theater group, both on stage and helping back stage, and I also belong to two exercise groups in the area. Currently, I am participating with a community beautification project within my neighborhood. All of these projects have been very rewarding and a nice social outlet for me. While not intended, it is amazing how social contacts can come back to reward the agency. Some of our volunteers and board members have been recruited through my social contacts.

What advice do you have for someone contemplating a career in gerontology? In a professional position similar to your current position?

Talk with a person already in that role. We are very approachable and would always be willing to talk about our responsibilities. It is important to truly seek out opportunities of working for or volunteering with older adults before graduation to confirm that it is the elderly population that interests you. If it is administration of an older adult organization or agency that is appealing to you, I believe it is important to first work in a social work position or with a direct service program before moving into administration. This will help give you an understanding and insight for those working for you when you do move into administration.

Dance/Movement Therapist (DMT)

Basic Description: Dance/Movement Therapy (DMT) is the psychotherapeutic use of dance and movement as a process and tool to assist and support integration of an individual's physical, cognitive, emotional, and social aspects of life. DMT is one of several creative arts therapies used with older adults to help improve their self-esteem, body image, balance, communication, and relationships; gain new insights into both positive and negative behaviors; and cope with the problems they face in one or more aspects of their lives. DMTs use movement expressed through dance as an observational and assessment tool and as a therapeutic and intervention process. Use of the language of the body—not just verbal communication—is a unique asset of DMTs. They usually work with both individual clients and groups.

Education and Experience Requirements: A master's degree in dance/movement therapy from an American Dance Therapy Association (ADTA)-approved program is required. Graduate students accepted for a DMT master's program usually have a bachelor's degree in liberal arts, extensive dance experience, and some coursework in psychology. Gerontology coursework or a degree component is encouraged for those who intend to work primarily with older adult clients.

Certification, Licensure, and Continuing Education Requirements: Dance Therapist Registered (DTR) requires a DMT master's degree with 700 hours of supervised clinical internship. An Academy of Dance Therapists Registered (ADTR) requires 3,640 hours of ADTR-supervised clinical work in an agency, institution, or special school and approval of the ADTA's credentials committee.

Core Competencies and Skills Needed:
* Working knowledge of aging processes and how they impact the body's ability to move
* Working knowledge of psychotherapeutic, counseling, and rehabilitation interventions and strategies
* Self-discipline

- Good interpersonal skills
- Good observation and assessment skills specific to dance/movement therapy
- Physically and emotionally fit

Compensation: This varies by one's education, experience, level of registration, and the nature of the workplace.

Workplace(s): These include long-term care and assisted living facilities, hospitals/medical centers, wellness centers, alternative health care centers and programs, substance abuse and chemical dependency treatment facilities and centers, counseling centers, senior centers, retirement communities and residences, crisis centers, and medical and psychiatric rehabilitation centers.

Employment Outlook: Limited—primarily due to a limited number of ADTA-approved master's degree programs (only five programs currently exist at colleges in Colorado, Illinois, New Hampshire, New York, and Pennsylvania). This outlook may be improved by increased interest in wellness and fitness among persons now entering elderhood.

Related Professional Organizations and Web Sites:
- American Dance Therapy Association (ADTA): www.adta.org
- National Coalition of Creative Arts Therapies Associations (NCCATA): www.nccata.org

---

Deputy Director, Area Agency on Aging

Basic Description: The deputy director of an Area Agency on Aging (AAA) is a member of the administrative team responsible for the planning, delivery, and evaluation of programs and services mandated by the Older Americans Act. Specific responsibilities of a deputy director may include oversight of day-to-day operations, personnel management (recruitment, hiring, supervision, evaluation, and discipline), development and maintenance of information and technology systems, development and management of operational budgets, preparation of grant proposals, and liaison with county units on aging and other human service agencies in the AAA's multicounty service area.

Education and Experience Requirements: A master's degree in social work, public administration, business administration, or related fields is required. Education or training in accounting and computer technology is strongly recommended. At least some coursework in gerontology is desirable. Employers also usually require 3–5 years of prior administrative experience in human services and/or an aging agency.

Certification, Licensure, and Continuing Education Requirements: None is required, but staying current with changes in policies on aging and regulations related to delivery of programs and services to older adults is vital.

Core Competencies and Skills Needed:
- Personnel assessment and management skills
- Information technology expertise
- Computer systems skills related to managing computer networks
- Policy development knowledge and skills
- Good written and oral communication skills, including public speaking
- Good interpersonal communication skills
- Knowledge of budgets and accounting processes
- Able to work collaboratively with other agencies
- Familiar with grant writing process (some experience preferred)

Compensation: This varies by state, factors related to the specific coverage area of the AAA, and continued funding of AAA programs and services from federal, state, regional, and county sources.

Workplace(s): This is typically the AAA regional office, usually located in the county in the AAA's coverage area with the largest elderly population.

Employment Outlook: Good—but limited in number per state and by the tendency toward longevity in position.

Related Professional Organizations and Web Sites:
- National Association of Area Agencies on Aging (n4a): www.n4a.org
- Administration on Aging (AoA): www.aaa.gov
- State organization for Directors of Area Agencies on Aging

An Interview with Robert C. Schlueter, Deputy Director & Chief Information Officer, Area Agency on Aging

What is your educational background in gerontology and other disciplines or professional fields? What formal credentials (e.g., completed degrees, certification) do you hold in these fields?

I earned bachelor's degrees in sociology (BS) and philosophy (BPh). My educational background in gerontology and the skills I use in my job today have been obtained mostly on the job. I worked in adult education programs in the past. My past employment positions involved extensive public presentations on initiatives; group dynamics; program development, including the development of budgets and staff; and staff management.

Briefly describe your gerontology-related career path.

Twenty years ago I was hired by the Area Agency on Aging to manage several of their employment services programs. I agreed to accept the position if they would involve me in other areas of the agency's work related to the elderly population. The rest is history. I have always enjoyed working with older persons, probably because my parents had kids late and I grew up around many very old people who were still active and giving back to their community in many positive ways.

How did you first become interested in your current professional position?

I am a social worker at heart. When I resigned from a job in government procurement that I was not fond of, I kept up an active search for an opportunity with some of the local private and public organizations and agencies that were involved in helping people put their lives back together or to work through problems related to bureaucratic indifference. My interest always involved working with and helping people, so I focused on the many opportunities that would offer this type of experience.

What are the most rewarding aspects of your career?

There are many. It is important to appreciate the little victories in this field. I can see in their eyes and feel in their hearts when I have made a positive difference in others' lives. I must appreciate the little victories, because the big ones are few and far between. I find it very rewarding that by improving one person's life, I am making the entire community a little bit better for all of us. There are many ways a positive difference can be made in someone's life, so it is just important for me to go out there and make it happen.

What are the most challenging aspects of your career?

Bureaucratic red tape and the inability for policymakers at the state and federal levels to understand what is really happening "on the street" is very frustrating and challenging because it affects so often the ease with which we can get our jobs completed successfully. Human beings, by their very nature, offer up the most positively exciting and, at the same time, the most heart-wrenchingly difficult situations we work with at the AAA. It is extremely challenging to be consistent and understanding day after day. It would be easy to give up helping if I was keeping score as to the successes vs. the failures. People want to know that I am there to help them with the same positive ability every day. Keeping positive and looking at new ways to do old things is very challenging.

Describe a typical workday in your current professional position.

I arrive around 7 a.m. and make sure that all of the technology equipment is working properly, because the staff depends on it every day to be able to complete their work. Every day brings a problem or two technology-wise that needs to be addressed. There are also weekly reports and ongoing meetings with staff that are consistent week after week. Many times, I need to address personnel issues that are as different as we are people. In times of financial difficulties, such as now, we constantly are looking at our budgets to identify ways to take care of our clients and also our staff in the best way possible. My job has me sitting on many committees around the ten counties that we serve, so a great deal of time each week is spent attending these meetings and working on issues like interagency collaboration, housing, transportation, and budgets.

I also work with various organizational boards to assist them in their function and operations. I usually leave the office before 6 p.m.

How do you balance career and other aspects of your life?

It is important for me to leave the work at the office and enjoy my time with family and friends outside of my work world. Most of my professional responsibilities are not crisis-related, so this "leave it at the office" effort is not hard to accomplish. I have found over the years, however, that the information I obtain for others professionally often becomes helpful to me in my own personal life or in the life of someone close to me. I believe strongly that it is important to have a solid, well-rounded lifestyle outside of the work place. My life outside of the workplace represents much more about whom I am and what I am like as a human being. It is important for my wife and me to be physically and mentally healthy and active. To achieve this, I believe that an awareness of where the professional job starts and ends is important.

What advice do you have for someone contemplating a career in gerontology? In a professional position similar to your current position?

We desperately need more professionals in the field of gerontology, especially in the medical fields. I have never had a job that I have enjoyed so much or where I felt like I was making such a significant positive change in our lives. It is important to understand that we will not solve all of the problems of our aging community, but that's not our job. Our job is to make a difference one little step at a time. All those steps lead up to a wonderful adventure over time. Although adequate salaries are available, I don't believe that there are many high paying jobs in the field of gerontology at this time. In today's administration job market, it is more important than ever to obtain either a Master's of Social Work (MSW) degree or an advanced degree in public administration or business. It is also very helpful to have a background in basic accounting and general computer software application skills. There are lots of opportunities to advance your accounting skills on the job, but the advanced social work or business degree is a "must have" to get your foot in the door of an Area Agency on Aging or similar agency. If you are interested in the academic side or research side of gerontology, then it is advisable to obtain a PhD in your specific interest area. The competition for jobs at an Area Agency on Aging and similar agencies is strong, so the more prepared you are on the academic side, the more doors that will be open for you to start that career in gerontology.

Drama Therapist/Registered Drama Therapist (RDT)

Basic Description: Drama Therapists and Registered Drama Therapists (RDTs) intentionally employ the processes of drama or theater (e.g., improvisation, storytelling or enactment, theater games, puppetry, role-playing, pantomime, mask work, theatrical production) to help their clients and patients meet individual or group therapeutic goals. To identify appropriate prevention, intervention, and treatment goals, they first assess clients' needs. Next, they devise a plan of action and use appropriate strategies to help their clients build interpersonal and personal skills, change negative or inappropriate behaviors, integrate their physical and emotional selves, and achieve personal mental and emotional growth. Text (e.g., literary dialogues, poetry, play scripts), performance, and ritual are among the "tools of trade" used by drama therapists. Also, drama therapists sometimes work collaboratively with professionals from other creative arts (e.g., music, dance/movement, and art therapy) to facilitate positive outcomes for their clients.

Education and Experience Requirements: This occupation requires a master's or doctoral degree in drama therapy from a program accredited by the National Association for Drama Therapy (NADT) or a master's or doctoral degree in theater or a mental health profession, with additional in-depth training in drama therapy, through NADT's alternative training program that is supervised by a board-certified registered drama therapist (RDT-BCT).

Certification, Licensure, and Continuing Education Requirements: The RDT designation requires completion of 500 hours of drama/theater experience, an on-site RDT-supervised internship in drama therapy, and 1000 hours of drama therapy experience.

Core Competencies and Skills Needed:
* Demonstrated competence in use of an array of drama/theater processes with diverse clients
* Commitment to patient-centered care
* Excellent interpersonal and communication skills
* Knowledge of theories related to personality and group processes

- Ability to be creative and innovative
- Ability to blend verbal and nonverbal components of drama therapy
- Ability to involve sometimes reluctant participants in therapy processes

Compensation: This varies by education, experience, registration as a RDT, type of professional practice, and the nature of the employment setting. Some positions may be part-time and wage-based or on a fee-for-service basis.

Workplace(s): These include mental health facilities, hospitals, substance abuse treatment centers, adult day care centers, correctional facilities, shelters, long-term care and assisted living facilities, private practice settings, corporations, theaters, housing projects, medical schools, training organizations, memory loss/dementia care programs and residential settings, senior centers, and other organizations or programs for older adults.

Employment Outlook: Limited—but the potential for improvement exists with the anticipated growth in the older adult population and as elders become more comfortable with seeking or accepting therapeutic intervention and treatment.

Related Professional Organizations and Web Sites:
- National Association for Drama Therapy (NADT): www.nadt.org
- National Coalition of Creative Arts Therapies Association (NCCATA): www.nccata.org

Driver Rehabilitation Specialist (DRS)

Basic Description: Driver Rehabilitation Specialists (DRS) provide driver rehabilitation services for individuals who are disabled, but are still able to drive if appropriate rehabilitation, equipment, and support is made available. A DRS first does clinical (predriving) evaluations and/or behind the wheel driving evaluations before developing and implementing a driving rehabilitation or mobility intervention plan specific to the client's needs. This plan may include recommendations for adaptive equipment, counseling related to a transitional return to driving, training toward the goal of driving independence, or identification of alternative transportation programs. The Association of Driving Rehabilitation Specialists (ADED) currently is the credentialing agency. While driver rehabilitation specialists come from many professional fields, many are occupational therapists. The American Occupational Therapy Association (AOTA) offers a Specialty Certificate in Driving and Community Mobility to occupational therapists (OTs) and occupational therapy assistants (OTAs) who meet certification eligibility requirements.

Education and Experience Requirements: Candidates are eligible for the Driver Rehabilitation Specialist Certification (CDRS) exam if they meet one of the following educational and/or experience requirements specified by the ADED:
- Four-year undergraduate degree or higher in health-related field,* plus 1 year of full-time work experience in a degree field and 1 additional year of full-time work experience in driver rehabilitation
- Two-year degree in health-related field,* plus 1 year full-time work experience in a degree field and 3 additional years of full-time work experience in driver rehabilitation
- Four-year undergraduate degree or higher, with a major or minor in traffic safety and/or driver and traffic safety endorsement, plus 1 year full-time of work experience in traffic safety and 2 additional years of full-time work experience in driver rehabilitation
- Five years of full-time work experience in the field of driver rehabilitation

Certification, Licensure, and Continuing Education Requirements: DRS certification (which is good for three years) is granted to candidates who meet specified education and/or work experience requirements, pay the required examination and application processing fees, and pass the CDRS exam. Recertification is based on the accumulation of continuing education credits (points) for approved professional activities. Candidates must possess a valid driver's license in the state where the practice occurs.

Core Competencies and Skills Needed:
- Excellent personal driving skills
- Knowledge of relevant state laws
- Good written and oral communication skills
- Knowledge of and competence in administering the required clinical and behind the wheel driving evaluations
- Understanding of the various disabilities experienced by clients

---

*Health-related fields include occupational therapy, physical therapy, kinesiotherapy, speech-language pathology, therapeutic recreation, or other fields approved by the ADED Certification Committee

- Good teaching and training skills
- Patience

Compensation: This varies by the type of professional practice, the nature of the workplace and employing agency, one's educational background, the amount and type of work experience, and the geographical location.

Workplace(s): These include rehabilitation clinics, hospitals/medical centers, organizations that offer driver retraining programs (e.g., AARP's 55 and Alive program), state departments of motor vehicles, and senior centers.

Employment Outlook: Good—with increasing opportunities as governmental programs are made available to meet the mobility and transportation needs of the rapidly growing older adult population.

Related Professional Organizations and Web Sites:
- Association for Driver Rehabilitation Specialists (ADED): http://aded.net
- American Occupational Therapy Association (AOTA): www.aota.org

Educational Gerontologist

Basic Description: Education about elders, education for elders, and education by elders is how Howard Y. McClusky defined educational gerontology, the field for which he is considered to be the founding father. From this perspective, educational gerontologists would include gerontology and geriatrics program administrators and faculty members in higher education, administrators and facilitators of older learner programs in a variety of settings, and older adults who serve as teachers and facilitators of learning for other older adults. In regard to professional positions, however, the largest numbers of positions are held by those who are part of the first two of these categories, although none hold a degree in educational gerontology and most use a title other than educational gerontologist. Instead, educational gerontologists come from a vast array of disciplines and professional fields. Regardless of their educational backgrounds, they develop, implement, and evaluate educational programs, courses, and other learning experiences about aging in a wide variety of settings, including higher education, professional schools, K-12 schools, adult and community education programs, institutes for learning in retirement and other older learner programs, religious facilities, and many other settings. They prepare educational materials about aging and older adults, including textbooks, professional handbooks and encyclopedias, journal articles, print materials for consumption by the general public, educational films, and other audiovisual teaching/learning tools. Some educational gerontologists are theorists and researchers who work to better understand adult learning processes and to develop curriculum models and methodologies that are appropriate for adult learners.

Education and Experience Requirements: These vary by the type of position and the nature of the employment setting. For most administrative and teaching positions in higher education, including professional schools, a doctoral degree in a discipline (such as anthropology, sociology, psychology, or biology), or in a professional field (such as social work, geriatric medicine, nursing, physical or occupational therapy, interior design, family studies, or gerontology) is required. A minimum of a bachelor's degree is required for teaching K-12 and credit-granting adult and community education program courses.

Certification, Licensure, and Continuing Education Requirements: Educational gerontologists must meet certification and licensure requirements set by the state in which the professional practice occurs and/or by the employing institution, organization, or agency. Continuing education is frequently required for tenure and promotion or advancement from teaching to administrative positions.

Core Competencies and Skills Needed:
- Updated understanding of research-based knowledge about aging processes and older adult population
- Specialized education and/or training in subject matter to be taught
- Good working knowledge of adult learning theories and methodologies
- Demonstrated ability to develop, implement, and evaluate appropriate curriculum design and methodologies
- Familiarity with relevant professional resources
- Good working knowledge of educational technology specific to teaching or administrative assignment
- Good interpersonal skills
- Good communication skills (written, oral, listening)

Compensation: This varies by education, experience, type of position and the level of responsibility, the nature of the employment setting, and the geographical location. Some positions are part-time and may be paid by hourly wage, rather than salary.

Workplace(s): These include community colleges, colleges, universities, professional schools; K-12 public and private schools, school district adult and community education programs and other community-based educational programs and services; institutes for learning in retirement and other older learner programs; visiting professor and adjunct teaching positions in higher education; and consulting opportunities in corporate and other non-educational settings.

Employment Outlook: Excellent—due to the anticipated rapid growth of the older population and the expanding number of venues for older learner programs and services.

Related Professional Organizations and Web Sites:
- American Association for Adult and Continuing Education (AAACE): www.aaace.org
- Association for Gerontology in Higher Education (AGHE): www.aghe.org
- Lifetime Education and Renewal Network (LEARN), American Society on Aging (ASA): www.asaging.org

Education & Curriculum Specialist, Lifelong Learning Program/Institute

Basic Description: Lifelong learning institutes provide participant-driven and highly interactive learning programs and services for active older adults (usually at least 50 years of age or older; some programs specify 60 or 65 and older). Education & Curriculum Specialists are responsible for recruitment of institute members and participants; assessment of learning needs and interests; development of the curriculum; promotion, implementation, facilitation, oversight, and evaluation of institute/program offerings; and recruitment, training, and oversight of program volunteers and hosts. In some settings the specialist also may be the institute director or deputy director, with responsibility for administrative tasks such as budgeting, personnel administration, fundraising, and grants management. Other tasks of the specialist may include serving as a link to other lifelong learning opportunities in the community; establishing and maintaining private and public partnerships; serving as the institute's liaison with relevant community organizations, agencies, and governing bodies; convening a voluntary advisory council and serving as an ad hoc member on its committees; offering outreach programming to underserved populations in the institute's service area; creating opportunities for intergenerational programs and services; and establishing and monitoring a dedicated computer area for use with institute programs.

Education and Experience Requirements: A master's degree in adult education, educational gerontology, instructional technology, community leadership, or a closely related field is required. Coursework in gerontology, adult or life course development, intergenerational studies, curriculum development, community leadership, and/or program development is strongly recommended.

Certification, Licensure, and Continuing Education Requirements: These professionals must meet licensure and continuing education requirements of their primary profession, the employing agency, and that state in which the practice occurs. Optional certifications are available through continuing education opportunities.

Core Competencies and Skills Needed:
- Working knowledge of adult/older adult learning theories and methodologies
- Working knowledge of curriculum development and implementation for adult learners
- Excellent written and oral communication skills; excellent listening skills
- Working knowledge of needs and interest assessment tools and processes
- Working knowledge of program evaluation tools and processes
- Ability to work with learners from diverse educational, social, and cultural backgrounds
- Ability to work collaboratively with partners from other community organizations and agencies
- Good organizational skills; ability to multitask
- Computer and educational technology literacy
- Resourceful and innovative
- Love of learning

Compensation: This varies by one's education, experience, the nature of the employment setting, and the geographical location. Some positions may be part-time or combined with responsibilities of another position.

Workplace(s): These include libraries, senior centers, institutes for learning in retirement (academic and non-academic), adult and community education programs, faith-based communities, academic institutions, and wellness and holistic health centers.

Employment Outlook: Promising—however, demand has not yet been determined for this emerging form of adult/older adult education.

Related Professional Organizations and Web Sites:

- American Association for Adult and Continuing Education (AAACE): www.aaace.org
- Elderhostel Institute Network of Institutes for Learning in Retirement: www.elderhostel.org/ein/
- Learning Resources Network (LERN): www.lern.org
- Lifelong Access Libraries: www.lifelonglibraries.org
- Lifetime Education and Renewal Network (LEARN), American Society on Aging (ASA): www.asaging.org
- National Community Education Association (NCEA): www.ncea.com
- National Resource Center for Osher Lifelong Learning Institutes (OLLI): www.usm.maine.edu/olli/national

An Interview with Linda Hayes Gallegos, Education & Curriculum Specialist, Public Library Lifelong Learning Institute

What is your educational background in gerontology and other disciplines or professional fields? What formal credentials (e.g., completed degrees, certification) do you hold in these fields?

My BA is in social psychology and my MA is in instructional technology (design of adult education and training programs). I have no formal educational background in gerontology, but I continually upgrade my skills and knowledge. Most recently, I was selected as a Fellow for the first Lifelong Access Libraries Summer Institute and I attended the "The Art of Age-ing: The Gift of Sage-ing" intensive workshop (programming that encourages and supports conscious aging) offered by the Sage-ing Guild. I am also a certified spellbinder (storytelling in the schools), laughter leader (facilitating group laughter), and conversations game facilitator (group sharing of personal insights and wisdom). Although these may seem a bit off the wall at first glance, they are some of our more popular programs, as they foster active and engaged aging, intergenerational relationships, community building, and personal development.

Briefly describe your gerontology-related career path.

My experience in gerontology was acquired while serving as a companion for more than seven years to a friend living in a retirement community. As a member of the next cohort of older adults, I am passionate about my active engagement in redefining the aging process and inventing our Third Age. While working as a Program Coordinator for the Division of Continuing Education at the University of Central Florida, it became clear that I enjoyed being "in front of the classroom" much more than "behind the desk," so I took advantage of the free tuition benefit and completed my master's degree. I was already working with adults and a career in Instructional Technology provided me with the skills and knowledge to design and implement adult education programs—not just coordinate them. After five years as an independent consultant, I realized the importance of being in a place where my work could have a greater impact on a larger group of people, which is how I came to my current position as education and curriculum specialist at this library. My understanding of older adults continues to grow as I interact with them on a daily basis through our various programs.

How did you first become interested in your current professional position?

As a long-time educator of many subjects, including English/Spanish as a second language, Mexican folk dancing, and energy healing, my personal commitment has always been to support others in their growth process by providing them with opportunities, knowledge, skills, and tools to reach their full potential and find life satisfaction, no matter their age. I am especially interested in tapping the potential of the incoming group of older adults. When this new and innovative position as education and curriculum specialist for the library's lifelong learning institute became available, I saw it as the perfect place to reach people of all ages, but especially those lifetime learners in the 50+ demographic. Working within a public library is particularly rewarding because it is a neutral and familiar space to many, open and accessible to all, and in the process of becoming not only an information center, but also an education and community center—a place to engage its patrons and build community.

What are the most rewarding aspects of your career?

Here are but a few of the rewards from my current career position: witnessing the positive life changes our participants experience, especially those who attend the vital living programs; bringing new ideas and perspectives to the library environment and the community at large; creating opportunities for community members to connect and make new friends, share experiences and wisdom, exchange new ideas and perspectives, and explore different life choices—in short, being a catalyst for change and transformation.

What are the most challenging aspects of your career?

Because we are charting new territory with this unique career option within the system of libraries nationwide, our challenge lies in attracting the attention, interest and support not only of our target population, but of the community as a whole. This directly affects the amount of resources available to accomplish all that could and should be done. My second challenge is keeping my enthusiasm and desire to provide a full array of programs from completely taking over my personal life.

Describe a typical workday in your current professional position.

The exciting thing about this career is that there is no "typical" day. The depth and breadth of activities keep my work life from getting boring; knowledge and skills in many areas are required as I execute multiple roles. To give you an idea of the diverse activities I am involved in on a daily basis, I will share a characteristic day. I begin the day attending the Community Partnerships monthly breakfast at the County Office on Aging to connect with area organizations that service older adults and to share what we are doing at the Lifelong Learning Institute. Back at the office, I host the weekly "Notables of Our Time" program. Next, I head over to city hall to lead a Laughter Club activity for city employees. In the afternoon, I send e-mail to confirm the participation of alternative healing practitioners at next month's Complementary Therapies Wellness Fair, call potential presenters for the Teachers' Conference to be held in the summer, and create flyers for these programs. I also participate in a creative problem-solving process to determine how to attract and retain volunteers. In the evening, I facilitate an ElderCare class and send out an e-mail blast with next week's programs.

How do you balance career and other aspects of your life?

This is a major challenge! I never thought I would ever say it, but, at the present time, my career is my life; it also is my life's purpose, so it is meaningful and fulfilling. I incorporate much of my personal life into this position, since so many of my own interests reflect those of our target population. We are also slowly building an active group of volunteers who serve as program facilitators and hosts; this takes some stress off of me.

What advice do you have for someone contemplating a career in gerontology? In a professional position similar to your current position?

This can be a highly rewarding and satisfying career. If your passion includes improving the quality of life of others, this career most definitely provides you with opportunities to have an impact on many lives through diverse and varied services and program offerings that address the needs, issues, concerns, curiosity, and appetite for learning of midlife adults and active elders. The key skills you will need are a love of working with people and a willingness to try new things.

Elder Advocate, Area Agency on Aging

Basic Description: An Elder Advocate employed by an Area Agency on Aging (AAA) is responsible for working with older adults and their caregivers to provide information, advocacy, and assistance through a variety of means that include: conducting assessments, monitoring needs, connecting individuals with benefit programs, counseling, and making referrals to appropriate community resources. In some AAAs this position is titled Information & Referral Specialist, Care/Case Manager, or Caseworker, however, the responsibilities of these positions may vary from those identified here for an elder advocate. Elder advocate may also refer to persons who work in other aspects of the field of gerontology (see Ombudsperson/Elder Advocate), including long-term care settings, physical and mental health centers, assisted living facilities, adult protective services, legal/paralegal clinics, and other organizations or agencies where a professional is responsible for advocating for and/or on behalf of clients.

Education and Experience Requirements: A Master's degree in Social Work or a closely related professional field is required. Gerontology coursework or a degree component is strongly recommended as part of undergraduate or graduate studies.

Certification, Licensure, and Continuing Education Requirements: Elder advocates must meet licensure requirements in the state where the practice occurs. Certification and continuing education relevant to professional practice is strongly encouraged and may be required for licensure in some states.

Core Competencies and Skills Needed:
- Knowledgeable about entitlement and benefit programs and services for older adults
- Knowledgeable about community programs for and issues facing older people in the AAA service area
- Ability to manage multiple concurrent priorities
- Flexibility in handling diverse situations and clients

- Strong interpersonal skills
- Knowledge of appropriate assessment tools and procedures
- Creative and innovative
- Good problem-solving skills
- Good listener; good oral and written communication skills
- Ability to be and stay organized

Compensation: This varies by one's education, experience, the specific job tasks assigned to the position, the level of responsibility within the agency, and the geographic location.

Workplace(s): This is typically the AAA regional office, which is usually located in the county in the AAA's coverage area with the largest elderly population.

Employment Outlook: Excellent—due to the anticipated increase in demand as the elderly population grows over the next several decades.

Related Professional Organizations and Web Sites:
- National Association of Area Agencies on Aging (n4a): www.n4a.org
- Administration on Aging (AoA): www.aoa.gov
- National Association of Social Workers (NASW): www.nasw.org

An Interview with Jennifer Illig, Elder Advocate, Area Agency on Aging

What is your educational background in gerontology and other disciplines or professional fields? What formal credentials (e.g., completed degrees, certification) do you hold in these fields?

I have a Master's of Social Work (MSW) degree, with concentrations in Interpersonal Practice and Aging and Families, and a Specialist in Aging Certificate. I was fortunate to be a recipient of a Geriatric Fellowship for my graduate work. I also have a Bachelor of Science (BS) in Psychology with a Minor in Gerontology. I am currently a Licensed Master Social Worker (LMSW) in the State of Maine.

Briefly describe your gerontology-related career path.

As an undergraduate, I chose to major in Psychology and minor in Gerontology. I knew that I wanted to work with older people but debated between research and direct practice. In the end, it was direct practice that I was most passionate about. My minor was a starting point, but I wanted more education in gerontology; therefore, I searched and applied to master's programs in social work that offered aging concentrations. During my graduate studies, I completed two internships. One was at a nonprofit agency that provided supportive services to keep elders in the community. It was, however, in my second internship with a State Health Insurance Program (SHIP), where I educated older adults and the larger community on Medicare, Medicaid, and Medicare Part D, that my interests really developed. Two months after graduation, I accepted this position as an Elder Advocate at an Agency on Aging (AAA) and I have now been here for more than a year.

How did you first become interested in your current professional position?

I was attracted to my current position because it involved working directly with elders, allowed me to build on my continued interest in health insurance counseling, and provided me the opportunity to learn about a variety of community resources that will be beneficial in future employment searches, if and when I leave my current position. In choosing my current position, it was also important to evaluate the whole package. The two positions I considered were not in my home state and I would be moving to places where I did not know many people. For me, then, it was not only important to find a job that was a good fit, but also a place where I would be comfortable living.

What are the most rewarding aspects of your career?

Many older adults and caregivers come to the AAA because they either do not know what resources are available or do not know enough to feel comfortable applying for a program. It is extremely rewarding to explain a benefit to someone that he or she may not have understood, but now considers an option and to know that this person has the information and understands it enough to make an informed choice. Some of the most rewarding (and frustrating) experiences that I have had involve working with people on a continuing basis. It is difficult advocating for people, working through setbacks with them, and trying to explain why it is taking so long to see a difference. If and when the desired result occurs, though, it is one of the most rewarding experiences. Finally, I am lucky to be able to interact with older people on a daily basis. While not every interaction is favorable, I enjoy working and having the opportunity to share experiences with these older clients.

What are the most challenging aspects of your career?

One of the most challenging aspects of my career is working in an environment where, at times, agencies do not work together to help the clients they are trying to serve. This is difficult because it creates resentment and barriers that reduce the quality of services. It is also challenging when I find that people are eligible for a benefit, but there are no resources left to provide the benefit. Another challenge is accepting that sometimes there are no "good" answers and the best that I can do is help people to understand their options and feel more comfortable with their decisions. Finally, it can be challenging to balance the competing demands of clients, their families, and the agency.

Describe a typical workday in your current professional position.

For me, a typical day involves a general routine but the issues that come up are extremely varied. I spend a great deal of time talking to clients, caregivers, and other professionals on the phone to connect them to resources and help them problem solve. I meet for individual appointments with caregivers and elders on a wide range of issues, such as applying for benefits, discussing housing options, providing health insurance counseling, appealing decisions, and answering questions about long-term care. I screen and assess clients' incoming needs, then determine and make appropriate referrals. I also complete home visits and work with some clients on a continuing basis. Twice a month, I attend a case review session with my supervisor and coworkers where I present and/or offer feedback for some of our more challenging cases.

How do you balance career and other aspects of your life?

Being new to the profession, it is sometimes challenging to balance career and other aspects of my life. It is important for me to be involved in things outside of work that I enjoy and look forward to, so that I can be distracted from work and allow myself time to recharge. Because the issues that I work with are often emotionally charged, however, it is not always easy to forget them—even when I am doing things that I enjoy. Oftentimes, it helps me to consider that the more I worry about work-related issues, the greater my chances of burnout and the less effective I will be at my job.

What advice do you have for someone contemplating a career in gerontology? In a professional position similar to your current position?

I first became interested in gerontology by being around older people. Although it sounds obvious for someone contemplating a career in gerontology, it could be helpful to volunteer/work with elders and to examine aging issues to find out if it is something that you enjoy. If you know that you want a career in gerontology, but do not know exactly what you want to do, explore different options and try not to feel limited to only traditional professions. For someone interested in geriatric social work, I would encourage you to examine several work settings where you can apply your social work skills with older people. Because social work is such a diverse field you will have many options. As a social worker, I have learned the importance of working with my coworkers. We all have varying degrees of knowledge on different topics and there is no way to be an expert on everything. My advice would be to continue learning things, but to also know who to go to when you have questions.

Elder Law Attorney
Certified Elder Law Attorney
Elder Care Attorney

Basic Description: Elder Law Attorneys specialize in the practice of law related to legal matters of specific concern to older/elderly persons, their families, caregivers, and legal representatives. These law matters include: health and personal care planning; premortem legal planning; fiduciary representation; legal capacity counseling; public benefits advice; advice on insurance matters; resident rights advocacy; housing counseling; employment and retirement advice; income, estate, and gift tax advice; public benefits advice; counseling related to age and/or disability discrimination in employment and housing; and litigation and administrative advocacy. A Certified Elder Law Attorney has enhanced knowledge, skills, experience, and proficiency in elder law practice and has met the requirements for certification set out by the National Elder Law Foundation (NELF). Certification, however, is voluntary and is not required for an attorney to practice elder law. An elder law attorney who specializes in matters specific to the care of elders who are at-risk due to physical and/or mental frailty may prefer to be called an Elder Care Attorney.

Education and Experience Requirements: This profession requires a law degree (JD) and coursework specific to the field and practice of elder law. Gerontology coursework is strongly recommended in an undergraduate degree or as continuing education addition to the law degree.

Certification, Licensure, and Continuing Education Requirements: To become a Certified Elder Law Attorney, a candidate must: be licensed to practice law in at least one state or the District of Columbia, have practiced law for the 5 years immediately prior to application for certification, be a member in good standing with the bars in all states where he or she is licensed, have averaged at least 16 hours per week in elder law practice, have handled at least 60 elder law matters during each of the 3 years immediately prior to application, have participated in at least 45 hours of continuing legal education in elder law during the preceding 3 years, submit five references from attorneys who can attest to his or her competence and qualifications in elder law, and sit for the certification examination within 2 years of filing the certification application. Certification is good for 5 years. Recertification requires the candidate to meet the same standards required for the original certification.

Core Competencies and Skills Needed:
- Ability to recognize issues of concern that arise during counseling and representation of older persons or their representatives on relevant law matters
- Familiarity with public and private, professional and non-legal resources and services that are available to meet the needs of older persons
- Ability to recognize professional conduct and ethical issues that arise during representation of older persons
- Good listening, oral and written communication skills

Compensation: This varies by the type of practice, the nature of the practice setting, one's education, experience, NELF certification, and geographical location.

Workplace(s): These include independent practices, law firms, medical centers or long-term care facilities, legal aid clinics, law schools, and consultation opportunities with health care systems, mental health facilities, and community-based public and private agencies that serve elders.

Employment Outlook: Excellent—with anticipated growth due to the increase in the elderly population and new laws and regulations that have legal implications for elders, their representatives, caregivers, and families.

Related Professional Organizations and Web Sites:
- American Bar Association (ABA): www.abanet.org
- ABA Commission on Law & Aging: www.abanet.org/aging
- National Elder Law Foundation (NELF): www.nelf.org
- National Academy of Elder Law Attorneys (NAELA): www.naela.com

An Interview with
Roxanne J. Chang,
Elder Care Attorney

What is your educational background in gerontology and other disciplines or professional fields? What formal credentials (e.g., completed degrees, certification) do you hold in these fields?

I have earned a Bachelor's degree in Psychology, a Graduate Certificate in Gerontology, a Master's degree in Clinical-Behavioral Psychology, and a Juris Doctor in Law. I am licensed in the State of Michigan as a Limited Licensed Psychologist and am a member of the State Bar of Michigan.

Briefly describe your gerontology-related career path.

I started out as a limited licensed psychologist providing mental health services for individuals in institutional long-term care settings and as a consultant in dementia care. I then became an elder care attorney.

How did you first become interested in your current professional position?

I have always had an interest in issues related to older adults, particularly Alzheimer's disease and related dementias. I learned of elder and special needs law when I was working as a psychologist and I met an attorney who specialized in those areas.

What are the most rewarding aspects of your career?

The most rewarding aspects of being an elder care attorney are the opportunities to advise and assist older adults and their families in advocating for quality care in the long-term care system and other aging related issues and to plan properly for long-term care. I also find it extremely rewarding to assist vulnerable adults and ensure that they are protected to the greatest degree possible while I'm also promoting independence and self-determination.

What are the most challenging aspects of your career?

The most challenging aspects are related to the barriers of quality care within the long-term care and legal system and the potential or actual abuse, neglect, or exploitation of a vulnerable adult.

Describe a typical workday in your current professional position.

A typical workday includes frequent meetings with clients at their homes or in long-term care facilities; conducting legal research; drafting court documents and pleadings; drafting estate planning documents; attending advocacy group meetings to address issues, such as improving long-term care, elder abuse, neglect, and financial exploitation; and providing feedback on proposed legislation, regulation, and policy.

How do you balance career and other aspects of your life?

I balance career and other aspects of my life by ensuring that I am creative, amused, bemused, mindful, and awake when completing my professional activities. In my personal time, I also enjoy art and attending events (such as the Burning Man Art Festival), listening to music, cooking, learning about wine, doing yoga, taking walks, working out, playing with my cats, and spending time with my friends and family.

What advice do you have for someone contemplating a career in gerontology? In a professional position similar to your current position?

I think that pursuing a career in gerontology is one where you get the best of both worlds—it is incredibly rewarding and the opportunities for employment and stability are vast. In order to be an effective elder care attorney, experience with the long-term care system, as well as issues related to dementia, are particularly important.

Foster Grandparent Program (FGP) Director
Foster Grandparent Program (FGP) Coordinator

Basic Description: The Foster Grandparent Program (FGP) is a Senior Corps Program affiliated with the Corporation for National and Community Service. Through FGP, persons 60 years of age and older work one-on-one with disabled or disadvantaged youth in schools and related settings. **FGP Directors** manage the overall operation of the program, including the following tasks: developing and monitoring the program budget; writing, monitoring and managing grants; supervising paid staff (FGP Coordinators and clerical staff); identifying volunteer stations that fit FGP guidelines and meet community needs in the program's service area; recruiting, training, placing, and evaluating volunteers (Foster Grandparents); maintaining open communication with and responding to issues, concerns, and problems that arise among program staff, volunteers, and volunteer station personnel. **FGP Coordinators** work directly with Foster Grandparents on a daily basis and assist the FGP Director with budget and grant preparation; volunteer recruitment, training and evaluation; maintenance of the required schedule, volunteer hours, performance and other records for individual volunteers; and other tasks as requested by the Director.

Education and Experience Requirements: The FGP Director position requires a bachelor's degree or higher in a related field (e.g., education, human development, social work); a master's degree is preferred by most employing agencies. Coursework or a degree component in gerontology and coursework in program management, or volunteer agency administration is desirable. The **FGP Coordinator** position also requires a bachelor's degree in a related field (e.g., education, human development, social work). Coursework or a degree component in gerontology is encouraged.

Certification, Licensure, and Continuing Education Requirements: Directors and coordinators must meet all state licensure requirements related to their base professional field. Continuing education requirements may be specified by their employing agency or FGP mandate.

Core Competencies and Skills Needed:

- Firm knowledge of state and federal policies, guidelines, and procedures for FGP
- Good organizational skills
- Good time and budget management skills
- Knowledge of school-based programs for disabled and disadvantaged youth
- Comfortable with working in disadvantaged communities or community settings
- Good interpersonal communication skills
- Grant writing skills

Compensation: This varies by type of position, the nature of the employing agency, and the geographical location. The position may be part-time or combined with another part-time position, such as directing or coordinating another older adult volunteer program or doing case/care management.

Workplace(s): These include county commissions on aging or other aging-specific human service agencies. Foster Grandparents are placed in worksites such as in daycare centers, Head Start programs, K-12 school classrooms, jail/prison education programs, and other settings that serve disadvantaged or disabled youth.

Employment Outlook: Moderate—but contingent upon continued FGP funding.

Related Professional Organizations and Web Sites:

- Corporation for National and Community Service: www.cns.gov
- National Association of Foster Grandparent Program Directors: http://nafgpd.theabramgroup.com

An Interview with
Mary Ann Mooradian,
Foster Grandparent & Senior
Companion Program Coordinator

What is your educational background in gerontology and other disciplines or professional fields? What formal credentials (e.g., completed degrees, certification) do you hold in these fields?

I have a Bachelor of Social Work (BSW) degree. My major was social work, with a minor in child development that had an emphasis in family studies.

Briefly describe your gerontology-related career path.

I have been in the field of gerontology for the past 23 years, all of which have been with the same county commission on aging, and working with the Foster Grandparent and Senior Companion Programs.

How did you first become interested in your current professional position?

I have always enjoyed the company of older adults; it goes back to when my grandmother lived with my family. I knew the person in the Foster Grandparent Program (FGP) Supervisor position, so I was very aware of the program. When the position opened, I applied for it and was fortunate to be selected. I served in that position for 18 years before stepping up to the position of Director for both the Foster Grandparent Program and Senior Companion Program (SCP).

What are the most rewarding aspects of your career?

The most rewarding aspect is knowing that I have had a small part in the wonderful things that our volunteers are doing to help meet the special needs of youth and frail older adults in our communities. It is also rewarding to see how these programs have enriched the lives of the volunteers themselves.

What are the most challenging aspects of your career?

The most challenging aspect is in the area of funding and budgeting for my programs. There is the constant threat to our funding at all levels—federal, state and local. I must maintain open communication and contact with our legislators and local officials to educate and inform them in the attempt to avoid a reduction in our program budget. I truly believe in our volunteers and what they are doing, so I will do all I can to keep these programs alive.

Describe a typical workday in your current professional position.

Gather information to complete monthly financial reports. Make phone calls to secure speakers for monthly in-service training. Work on memos to inform volunteers, site staff and advisory council members regarding program updates and funding status—put out a call to action. Make plans and delegate duties in preparation for our annual recognition event. Take phone calls from volunteers, site staff and others throughout the day. Check and respond to e-mail. Take time out to speak with volunteers who walk in to the office. Keep abreast of developments at the legislative level.

How do you balance career and other aspects of your life?

I am very fortunate to work for an agency that is very supportive of its employees. I try to stay organized and on top of things both at work and at home—I make a lot of lists. There are times when I will need to spend time beyond the typical work week to meet deadlines or deal with other issues that will affect my programs; my family at home is very understanding. I also take time out to spend time with friends and coworkers outside the office setting.

What advice do you have for someone contemplating a career in gerontology? In a professional position similar to your current position?

A career in gerontology is very rewarding and challenging. If someone is considering applying for a position similar to mine, I strongly encourage them to volunteer as much as they can for programs and services with an emphasis on serving the needs of older adults. If available to them, I suggest they attend conferences or trainings on volunteer management. I also encourage them to gather as much information as possible about working with grants and to attend workshops on grant writing.

Fundraiser
Development Director

Basic Description: Professionals in fundraising and development are responsible for the design, implementation, and evaluation of fund-raising programs (often called "campaigns") intended to supplement or enhance the basic operational budget of a nonprofit organization, agency, or facility. The funds raised may be for the general operational fund or earmarked for specific programs or special projects. Although the titles of Fundraiser and Development Director are sometimes used synonymously, the title of Fundraiser might be used for entry-level paid professionals and for volunteers for fundraising efforts. **Fundraisers** assist in the development of a fundraising campaign, make direct contact with potential donors through a variety of strategies, and report to the development director. Essentially, fundraisers are the "frontline" workers for a campaign. **Development Directors** are responsible for the development, planning, and execution of a development program that may include multiple fundraising campaigns and strategies. They identify and cultivate new and existing donors; implement the fund raising program so as to maximize the gift giving and stewardship for specific organization programs and projects; are responsible for gift management, fundraising events, and recognition of donors; maintain the development program database; create and/or oversee public and community relations, outreach, and marketing; create, oversee, and adhere to the development program budget; recruit, train, supervise, and evaluate development program staff members and volunteers; and report on development program activities to higher-level organizational administrators and boards. Some development directors have responsibilities related to the organization's grants program (see Grant Writer).

Education and Experience Requirements: **Fundraisers** need a bachelor's degree or higher in a field related to professional practice or equivalent work experience. Gerontology coursework or a degree component is encouraged. **Development Directors** require a master's degree or higher, preferably in a field related to professional practice, and at least 3-5 years relevant fundraising/development experience. Gerontology coursework or a degree component also is encouraged for directors.

Certification, Licensure, and Continuing Education Requirements:
Two voluntary certifications are available through the Association for Fundraising Professionals (AFP). To be eligible for the Certified Fund Raising Executive (CFRE), an individual must have at least 5 years of paid professional practice in fundraising and meet the minimum point requirements in four categories: education (continuing education workshops, seminars, conferences, and/or academic degree), professional practice (paid professional experience on a philanthropic fundraising staff or as a consultant to a nonprofit organization), professional performance (communications projects, management projects, and/or actual funds), and service (participation in professional and/or community organizations). Once these eligibility requirements are met, a candidate must pass the Computer-Based (CBT) exam, agree to adhere to the CFRE Donor Bill of Rights, and sign an agreement with the CFRE International Accountability Standards. Recertification is required every 3 years and is based on an update of education, professional practice, professional performance, and service activities. Advanced Certified Fundraising Executive (ACFRE) candidates must currently be working in the profession and have accumulated 10 or more years of professional fundraising experience. They must hold CFRE credentials and have been recertified at least once. They must have a BS/BA degree or equivalent, have completed at least 15 contact hours of senior-level management and 15 contact hours of senior-level leadership seminars/courses, have at least 5 hours of continuing education in fundraising ethics, hold membership and be active in at least one field-related professional organization, have completed volunteer service with at least one nonprofit organization, and adhere to the AFP's Code of Ethical Practice and Standards of Professional Practices and the Donor Bill of Rights. Upon successful completion of the written application attesting to the previous requirements, candidates must pass a multiple-choice exam, a portfolio review, and an oral peer review.

Core Competencies and Skills Needed:
- Thorough working knowledge of fundraising/development processes and strategies
- Excellent verbal and written communication skills; excellent oral presentation skills
- Excellent interpersonal skills
- Good organizational and administrative skills
- Demonstrated leadership skills (for development director); emerging leadership skills and ability to work well in a team (for fundraiser)
- Familiarity with relevant software, including spreadsheets and database management
- Positive personality
- Self-starter

Compensation: This varies by one's education, experience, level of certification, level of responsibility, and the nature of the employing agency/organization. Some positions may be part-time and wage-based or on a fee-for-service basis.

Workplace(s): These include community-based nonprofit organizations, agencies, and facilities that serve older persons; governmental agencies/ programs that serve and support older adults; and community-based foundations and organizations that raise funds to support programs and services for older adults.

Employment Outlook: Good—especially due to shifts in governmental funding priorities and budget reductions related to programs and services for older adults as the elderly population expands.

Related Professional Organizations and Web Sites:
- Association for Fundraising Professionals (AFP): www.afpnet.org
- Certified Fund Raising Executive Program (CFRE), Association for Fundraising Professionals: www.cfre.org

---

Geriatric Care Manager/ Professional Geriatric Care Manager (PGCM)

Basic Description: Geriatric Care Managers are health and human services professionals with backgrounds in nursing, social work, gerontology, or psychology whose private professional practice is based on issues of aging and elder care. Their clients are ill, frail, and disabled elders and their families. The goal of their practice is to help their clients to achieve maximum potential function. Geriatric care managers assess clients' needs, develop a plan of care that meets these needs, manage and coordinate the implementation of the plan, recommend plan adjustments as needed, and provide appropriate support to clients and their families. The specifics of the care plan, however, are not carried out directly by the care managers, but by the client, his or her family members, and other care providers stipulated in the care plan. A **Professional Geriatric Care Manager** (PGCM) is a member of the National Association of Professional Geriatric Care Managers (GCM) who has made a commitment to adhere to the GCM Standards of Practice and Pledge of Ethics. In providing their professional services, PGCMs might conduct care planning assessments and offer solutions to problems that are identified; screen, arrange, and monitor in-home help or other services; review financial, legal, or medical issues and make referrals to geriatric specialists; provide crisis intervention; assist with client relocation; serve as a liaison with family members at a distance; provide consumer education and advocacy; and connect clients and their caregivers to appropriate services. Some PGCMs have professional credentials and licenses that allow them to provide individual or family therapy, assist with financial management, serve as a conservator or guardian, and/or provide direct caregiving services.

Education and Experience Requirements: A bachelor's or master's degree in nursing, social work, gerontology, psychology, or a closely related human services profession is required. Gerontology coursework or a degree component is strongly recommended for those who do not have a degree in gerontology. Membership in relevant professional organizations is strongly encouraged.

Certification, Licensure, and Continuing Education Requirements: These professionals must meet all the requirements specified by the geriatric care manager's base profession and by federal, state, county, and local laws that govern the practice of care/case management. GCM recognizes the following certifications that indicate the care manager has additional training and/or experience: Care Manager Certified (CMC), Certified Care Manager (CCM), Certified Social Work Case Manager (C-SWCM), and Certified Advance Social Work Case Manager (C-ASWCM).

Core Competencies and Skills Needed:
- Commitment to client-centered practice, including client self-determination and provision of care to the entire "client system"
- Ability to maintain confidentiality
- Commitment to practice with integrity and ethical behavior
- Excellent written, listening, and oral communication skills
- Ability to translate medical and consumer information to clients in terms they understand
- Good working knowledge of care needs assessment tools and procedures
- Good working knowledge of laws and regulations that govern geriatric care/case management
- Familiar with medical care, human service, and aging organizations/agencies in the community

- Ability to work collaboratively and cooperatively with both client system and other professionals involved in the plan of care
- Willingness to seek supervision and/or consultation, as needed, to develop, coordinate and/or manage the care plan

Compensation: This varies by one's education, experience, the specific nature of the professional practice and practice setting, and the geographical location.

Workplace(s): Most geriatric care managers work in private or group practices and some serve as consultants to medical centers, long-term and assisted living facilities, mental health clinics, hospice programs and facilities, or agencies and organizations that serve older adults.

Employment Outlook: Excellent—with anticipated demand due to the rapid increase in the older adult population and more persons living long enough to require caregiving and care management needs.

Related Professional Organizations and Web Sites:
- National Association of Professional Geriatric Care Managers, Inc. (GCM): www.caremanager.org

Geriatric Dentist

Basic Description: Dentists diagnose and treat individual patients for conditions that affect the teeth, tongue, gums, lips, and jaws, and often are the first health care professionals to detect an array of other diseases, including diabetes, cancer, osteoporosis, and some cardiovascular problems. They may perform surgeries to repair, restore, and maintain teeth (e.g., dental implants), gums, and oral structures that were damaged or lost due to accidents, disease, and other traumas. Recently, dentists have become more involved in cosmetic dental procedures. Dentists also are involved in education and prevention programs to improve dental health for their patients in the communities where they practice. Some dentists with advanced education become researchers and faculty members in dental schools and allied health departments of colleges/universities. Geriatric dentists have acquired specialized knowledge about aging and work primarily with patients who are older adults, usually in private practice or through consultation with other medical and health care professionals; some become researchers or academicians. Increased interest in geriatric dentistry is evident in the creation of a Gerontology and Geriatrics Education Section within the American Dental Education Association (ADEA) and the Fellowship in Geriatric Dentistry by the American Society for Geriatric Dentistry (ASGD). In 2007 ASGD joined with two other organizations, the American Association of Hospital Dentists (AAHD) and the Academy of Dentistry for Persons with Disabilities (ADPD), to form a new joint organization, the Special Care Dentistry Association (SCDA). ASGD Fellows who complete additional requirements may achieve Diplomate status in Special Care Dentistry.

Education and Experience Requirements: Geriatric dentistry requires a Doctor of Dental Medicine (DDM) from an accredited dental school. Fellowship in the American Society for Geriatric Dentistry (ASGD) requires: completion of a 2-year postdoctoral education program focusing on geriatrics/geriatric dentistry and/or direct involvement for 2 years in academic, institutional community health, or clinical practice related to care of older adults; a minimum of 5 years of ASGD membership; documented completion of 100 hours of continuing education related to geriatrics/geriatric dentistry within past 5 years or comparable experience; and the successful completion of an oral exam administered by ASGD Fellowship Council members.

Certification, Licensure, and Continuing Education Requirements: Geriatric dentists must meet licensure requirements in the state where the professional practice occurs. Continuing education is required for license renewal in most states.

Core Competencies and Skills Needed:
- Commitment to evidence-based practice
- Scientific knowledge about aging processes, factors that influence individual aging, acute and chronic health conditions/diseases prevalent among elders in relation to dental health and dental care needs of older adults
- Keen visual memory
- Excellent judgment of space and shape
- High degree of manual dexterity
- Literacy related to computer applications for dental and geriatric dental practice
- Demonstrated ability to use technologies (e.g., digital radiography and laser systems) specific to dental care practice
- Good interpersonal and oral communication skills
- Good oral and body hygiene

Compensation: This varies by one's education, experience, attainment of Fellow and/or Diplomate status, type of professional practice, the nature of the employment setting, and the geographical location.

Workplace(s): These include individual or group private practices, institutional settings (e.g., long-term care and assisted living facilities), academia, and consultancies to community organizations, agencies, and programs that serve older adults.

Employment Outlook: Excellent—due to the anticipated rapid growth of the elderly population.

Related Professional Organizations and Web Sites:
- American Dental Association (ADA): www.ada.org
- Special Care Dentistry Association (SCDA): www.scdaonline.org
- American Dental Education Association (ADEA): www.adea.org
- American Student Dental Association (ASDA): www.asdanet.org
- Informal Interest Group on Oral Health, Gerontological Society of America (GSA): www.geron.org

Geriatric & Special Needs Population Manager, National Health-Related Professional Association

Basic Description: The Geriatric & Special Needs Population Manager is responsible for the following functions and tasks: the proposal, implementation, management, coordination, and evaluation of association programs for older persons and populations with special care needs; collaboration with internal units and external partners for the purposes of identifying resources and developing projects related to the professional education, public education, advocacy, and research needs of geriatric and other populations with special association-specific health care needs; and the provision of expertise on access to association-specific health care and the promotion of health care related to the mission of the association for geriatric and special needs populations.

Education and Experience Requirements: This position requires a bachelor's degree or higher in a health-related field. A master's or doctoral degree in an association-specific health care focus is strongly preferred. Five or more years of experience in a health care discipline/profession, public health, social services, or education environment is required and should include considerable experience in program development, implementation, and evaluation and in writing policy reports, white papers, grant proposals, and other communications and grantsmanship documents.

Certification, Licensure, and Continuing Education Requirements: This position requires licensure or certification in a health care or human services discipline.

Core Competencies and Skills Needed:
- Good working knowledge of federal and state legislation and regulations related to health care issues for geriatric and special needs populations
- Good working knowledge of health care access issues for geriatric and special needs populations
- Proficiency with relevant computer software and databases
- High level of competence in management of competing priorities and multitasking
- Excellent analytical and planning skills
- Excellent verbal and written communication skills
- Excellent presentation skills
- Ability to summarize; ability to prepare and deliver accurate and concise communications

Compensation: This depends primarily on one's education and experience.

Workplace(s): These are typically a national headquarters office that is usually located in a large metropolitan area (such as San Francisco, Chicago, New York City, Washington, DC).

Employment Outlook: Limited—due to the relatively small number of such organizations, but potential exists for additional positions as more associations at this level attempt to respond to the growth of the elderly population over the next few decades.

Related Professional Organizations and Web Sites:
Web sites for specific associations of interest, including medical, dental, allied health, public health, nursing, social work/medical social work and chronic disease-specific organizations

Geriatrician

Basic Description: Geriatric Medicine is a subspecialty of two medical special-izations—internal medicine and family medicine. The American Board of Internal Medicine (ABIM) and the American Board of Family Medicine (ABFM) offer a Certificate of Added Qualifications in Geriatric Medicine upon successful comple-tion of the Geriatric Medicine exam. Geriatricians are internists or family practitio-ners who have earned voluntary certification in geriatric medicine. They have been trained in the processes of aging and have acquired special diagnostic, therapeutic, preventive, and rehabilitative skills to use in their professional practice with elderly patients. The American Geriatrics Society (AGS) was the first medical organiza-tion to recognize the value of comprehensive assessment of elderly patients. This approach requires assessment by a team of medical and allied health profession-als (e.g., physicians, social workers, nurses, pharmacists, occupational therapists, physical therapists, dietitians, psychologists, psychiatrists) and other profession-als (e.g., spiritual advisors), who address the older person's physical, mental, and social needs from a holistic perspective. In 1994 the John A. Hartford Founda-tion launched the Geriatrics for Specialists Project to expand geriatric expertise in 10 surgical and related medical specialties: anesthesiology, emergency medicine, general surgery, gynecology, ophthalmology, orthopedic surgery, otolaryngology, physical medicine and rehabilitation, thoracic surgery, and urology.

Education and Experience Requirements: Geriatricians require a bachelor's degree (BA or BS), with a strong emphasis on basic sciences, a Doctor of Medicine degree (MD) from a medical school (undergraduate medical education, 4 years) accredited by the Liaison Committee of the Committee on Medical Education (LCCME), a residency program (graduate medical education, 3 years for internal medicine and family medicine), and a Fellowship (subspecialty training in geriatric medicine). A PhD may be required for geriatricians who become researchers or faculty members in medical schools or other institutions of higher education.

Certification, Licensure, and Continuing Education Requirements: Geriatricians require licensure to practice in the state or jurisdiction of the United States in which their professional practice occurs. Continuing Medical Education (CME) varies by state, professional organizations, and by medical staff organizations. The Certificate of Added Qualifications in Geriatric Medicine must be renewed periodically and may be accomplished through CME credit and retesting on the Geriatric Medicine exam.

Core Competencies and Skills Needed:

- Commitment to an interdisciplinary teamwork and ability to work well in a team process
- Commitment to practice of comprehensive geriatric assessment
- Commitment to a holistic health approach
- Good listener
- Excellent communication and interpersonal skills
- Patience
- Ability to work with and on behalf of patients, as well as their family members and other caregivers

Compensation: This varies by one's education, experience, specific type of practice, the nature of the practice setting, and the geographical location.

Workplace(s): These include private practices, medical care centers and hospitals, clinics, long-term care facilities, medical schools, colleges and universities, research centers and institutes, and consultancy practices (e.g., with hospice programs and facilities, assisted living facilities, healthcare "senior living" corporations).

Employment Outlook: Excellent—due to a growing national shortage of certified geriatricians and the need for more surgical and related specialists with geriatric-specific training.

Related Professional Organizations and Web Sites:

- American Medical Association (AMA): www.ama-assn.org
- American Geriatrics Society (AGS): www.americangeriatrics.org
- John A. Hartford Foundation: www.jhartfound.org

Gerontological Librarian
Older Adult Librarian

Basic Description: The work of librarians is usually a blend of user services, technical services, and administrative services. "User services" refers to librarians' direct work with patrons to help them find the information they need; these services include an analysis of the user's needs to identify appropriate information; a search for, acquisition, and provision of relevant information and resources; and instruction to develop the user's information access skills. "Technical services" refers to tasks such as the acquisition and preparation of materials for use by library patrons. "Administrative services" refers to tasks related to oversight, management, and planning of library facilities and services; negotiation of contracts for library services, materials, and equipment; hiring and supervision of staff; public relations; grants procurement and fundraising; and budget preparation. Recently, new professional roles have emerged for "special librarians," such as gerontological librarians and adult or older adult/senior services librarians. Gerontological librarians fulfill reference and bibliographer roles in a variety of settings (e.g., public city/county libraries, libraries or information centers in higher education, corporations and industries). Adult services and older adult librarians tailor library programs and services to meet the interests and needs of adult/older adult patrons. A new initiative and library services model, Lifelong Access Libraries, focuses on lifelong learning, meaningful activity, and civic engagement for active older adults.

Education and Experience Requirements: A master's degree in library and information studies (MLIS), library science (MLS), librarianship (ML), or an MA or MS in library/information studies from an American Library Association (ALA)-accredited program is required. Special librarians (e.g., gerontological librarians, older adult librarians) may need an additional graduate or professional degree or degree component. Coursework or a degree component in gerontology is strongly recommended.

Certification, Licensure, and Continuing Education Requirements: None are required, but the completion of a continuing education certificate program in aging studies or gerontology, and other position-related fields, is encouraged.

Core Competencies and Skills Needed:
- Understanding the changing interests and needs of older adults
- Service-oriented; passionate about helping people find the information and resources they need
- Knowledge of a broad variety of relevant scholarly and public information sources
- Strong computer skills; technological aptitude; capable of using an extensive array of electronic resources and communication technology
- Strong interpersonal and collaborative skills
- Strong oral and written communication skills
- Good listener
- Love of learning

Compensation: This varies by one's educational background, experience, level of responsibility, the nature of the employment setting, size of the library, full- or part-time positions, and geographical location.

Workplace(s): These include public city and county libraries or branch libraries and community college, college, and university libraries.

Employment Outlook: Good—opportunities for librarians are anticipated through 2014 due to the increase in the elderly population, the large number of anticipated retirements among current librarians, and the Lifelong Access Libraries initiative. Growth in employment for librarians, however, may be slower than average for all occupations due to budget constraints at all levels of government and the increased use of computerized information storage and retrieval systems.

Related Professional Organizations and Web Sites:
- American Library Association (ALA): www.ala.org
- Lifelong Access Libraries: www.lifelonglibraries.org
- Americans for Libraries Council: www.americansforlibraries.org
- U.S. Department of Labor, Bureau of Labor Statistics, Occupational Outlook Handbook: Librarians: www.bls.gov

An Interview with Richard Bray, Librarian & Director of Older Adult Services, County Library

What is your educational background in gerontology and other disciplines or professional fields? What formal credentials (e.g., completed degrees, certification) do you hold in these fields?

I have a Bachelor's Degree in Social Work Education and a Master's Degree in Library & Information Science. I was selected as a Fellow for the first Lifelong Learning Access Libraries Institute in 2006 and am currently enrolled in an institute for geriatric social work's online certificate in aging program.

Briefly describe your gerontology-related career path.

My undergraduate field work involved working with older Filipino Americans as a community organizer. Subsequent careers as an independent bookseller and nonprofit arts administrator included years of volunteering in local and national organizations whose participants included many older adult activists. Several of these efforts involved multigenerational activities regarding community and political issues. My transition to the public library profession was consistent with my ever-growing passion for connecting people, literature, and public service. One of my earlier librarian experiences involved collaborating with a local senior center in presenting multigenerational computer classes. I later became a branch library's senior services representative and, from there, to become the director of the county library's system-wide programs for older adults.

How did you first become interested in your current professional position?

I participated in a series of personal and career evaluations and the number one career on my outcomes list was "librarian"! Although I had served on the board of the Friends of the Chicago Public Library and had worked with and knew several librarians through my careers and volunteering, the thought of becoming a librarian had never occurred to me. At this point and with the help of some friends and colleagues, the decision to go to library school clicked.

What are the most rewarding aspects of your career?

Service to older adults, especially those in need, as well as the incredible learning experience I receive on a daily basis!

What are the most challenging aspects of your career?

Witnessing the cuts in funding for federal- and state-level services for older adults, caregivers, agencies, programs and services!

Describe a typical workday in your current professional position.

Most days will find me working with volunteers and responding to literary needs of homebound and institution-bound folks; working on current adult program and planning future programs; assisting library staff with providing library services to older adults; participating in person or electronically with community organizations I'm active in; purchasing library materials (books, DVDs, & more) of interest to a wide range of older adults; and viewing professional literature related to aging, gerontology, and library services.

How do you balance career and other aspects of your life?

The countless examples of "elder wisdom," compassion and humor I witness daily from folks we serve and coworkers contribute directly to a more relaxed and healthy "non-work" existence for me. I have spent most of the past 20 years as a primary caregiver for my brother and my mother plus dealing with the continuing challenges of a life-threatening disease. This career change into a full-time "gerontological librarian" has truly contributed to a more balanced path for me. I am a "pre-boomer" by six months and still an activist in my 60s, so it is not an exaggeration to say that the rewards and challenges of my career are truly a blessing for my continued laid-back and exciting personal life.

What advice do you have for someone contemplating a career in gerontology? In a professional position similar to your current position?

Whether you are considering your first career or you are in your 50s or 60s and interested in changing jobs, I think you will be forever grateful if you choose a career that combines gerontology and librarianship. Older adults are the fastest growing number of people going online, yet, due to their age, they still appreciate and welcome "face-to-face" contact and service. Work in a public library offers the best of both services. Also, as a librarian, you will be guaranteed training and retraining on the most advanced information technology systems. There are currently only a handful of public librarians country-wide whose primary job duty is working with older adults. The library profession—from the national to the state level and down to the smallest branch library—however, is recognizing this need, so entry-and mid-level positions are becoming available. If you are already a librarian, consider specializing in or expanding your work amongst older adults. People trust the library and are eager to collaborate with libraries on public programming and other partnering efforts. If you think you might enjoy working with older adults of all ages and from diverse backgrounds, and you also are interested in creative intergenerational programming and services, your job choices will be many. Active older persons are eager to partner with your library and are just waiting for librarians to join them. Go for it!

Gerontological/Geriatric Optometrist Low Vision Rehabilitation Specialist

Basic Description: Optometrists are primary eye care providers who examine the eye structure (internal and external) to diagnose vision conditions (e.g., near or farsightedness, presbyopia, astigmatism), eye diseases (e.g., cataracts, glaucoma, retinal disorders), and systemic diseases (e.g., diabetes, hypertension). Following diagnosis, they treat and manage diseases, injuries, and disorders of the visual system, eyes, and associated body structures. They are licensed to prescribe spectacle and contact lenses, low vision aid rehabilitation, vision therapy, and medications, and to perform some surgical procedures. Optometrists counsel patients regarding treatment plans and procedures. A unique aspect of optometry is the advanced study of optics—the science of light and vision—and extensive training related to corrective lens design, construction, application, and fitting. **Gerontological/Geriatric Optometrists** have completed an optional residency in gerontological/geriatric optometry and practice in settings where their primary clients are older adults. **Low Vision Rehabilitation Specialists** work with clients, including older adults, who are experiencing low vision problems that are treatable or correctable.

Education and Experience Requirements: A Doctor of Optometry (OD) degree from an accredited school/college of optometry is mandatory. Gerontology coursework or a degree component in a preprofessional undergraduate program is strongly recommended, and an optional residency in low vision rehabilitation and/or gerontological/geriatric optometry is strongly recommended.

Certification, Licensure, and Continuing Education Requirements: These professionals must meet state licensing requirements, including a state board examination and annual state-mandated continuing education requirements for optometrists.

Core Competencies and Skills Needed:

- Strong science foundation (including biology, chemistry, biochemistry, human anatomy, physiology, physics) in preprofessional undergraduate degree program
- Ability to differentiate between age-related visual changes and pathological eye diseases/condition and to understand the implications of each for the patient
- Commitment to patient-centered care
- Strong knowledge of the concepts and principles of the public health care system
- Good working knowledge of laws and regulations that govern optometric patient care
- Business management (e.g., personnel management, business finances)
- Good oral and written communication skills; good listening skills
- Commitment to ethical professional practice

Compensation: This varies by one's educational background, the type of practice, the nature of the employment setting, and the geographical location.

Workplace(s): These include private practices, multidisciplinary medical practices, hospitals, teaching institutions, research positions, community health centers, retail chains, military, public health or government services, and the ophthalmic industry.

Employment Outlook: Good—due to the current and future growth of the elderly population.

Related Professional Organizations and Web Sites:

- American Optometric Association (AOA): www.aoa.org
- American Academy of Optometry (AAO): www.aaopt.org

An Interview with
John E. Kaminski,
Optometrist/Low Vision Specialist

What is your educational background in gerontology and other disciplines or professional fields? What formal credentials (e.g., completed degrees, certification) do you hold in these fields?

I earned a Bachelor's of Science in Applied Biology degree in 1995, and concurrently completed the Doctor of Optometry and Graduate Interdisciplinary Specialization in Aging programs in 1999. In 2003, I was awarded certification as a Low Vision Specialist through the Michigan Optometric Association.

Briefly describe your gerontology-related career path.

My initial experience with work in geriatrics was during undergraduate school when I worked in a nursing home as a Certified Nurse Aid (CNA) and Certified Phlebotomist. While completing my Doctorate in Optometry, the Office of Gerontology Studies promoted the Graduate Interdisciplinary Specialization in Aging program to professional students in the medical, law, social work, optometry, dentistry, and pharmacy programs. I entered practice emphasizing geriatrics and low vision rehabilitation. Also, I have had academic opportunities to contribute to the gerontology program at a nearby university. Combining the clinical and academic experiences, I now present geriatric and aging courses at continuing education conferences around the country.

How did you first become interested in your current professional position?

Through mentorship—I knew someone who was an optometrist and his professionalism inspired me to become an optometrist. I observed different eye doctors in their offices to survey what appealed to my career goals. I spent time researching which subspecialties would be in need with the anticipated rapid growth of the elderly population. It was apparent to me early on in college that the health care needs of older adults are significantly underserved.

What are the most rewarding aspects of your career?

Helping others and making a difference in the lives of my patients. It is particularly rewarding to advocate for older adults in the health care system and provide a unique service, such as low vision rehabilitation. Working in optometry involves fewer interruptions from patient calls, a schedule that is predictable or family-friendly, and a fairly clean working environment. There are many facets—clinical care, business management, teaching, and research—of practicing optometry that I like.

What are the most challenging aspects of your career?

Managing a staff and the finances for my practice, including the paperwork and staffing costs associated with filing an ever-increasing number of insurance claims, is very challenging. Commercial optical and optometry chains that emphasize retail sales vs. patient care create an environment that is not conducive to caring for older adults or those with vision rehabilitation needs. It is a challenge to take care of underserved populations, such as elders or visually impaired individuals, in a patient-centered practice where an interdisciplinary approach is required for optimal care outcomes.

Describe a typical workday in your current professional position.

My work week is about 50 to 60 hours—Monday through Friday, 8 AM to 5 PM, with a half hour for lunch. I usually have a few hours of administrative tasks and/or paperwork before or after seeing patients each day. I will see about 15 patients of mixed ages in a given day. About 25% of my patients are older adults or individuals who have vision impairment, and these can be fairly complex cases. I'm out of the office occasionally to guest lecture at two universities and present courses at conferences. There also are several committees and research projects I participate in when I can find the time.

How do you balance career and other aspects of your life?

I make my own schedule so I can make time for special events, such as when my children are in school. I try to delegate as much work as possible to our office staff. My work week involves very few interruptions outside of normal office hours and I don't have to travel much. When I lecture at conferences, I bring my family and make a vacation out of it. It helps that I married another health care professional, who is understanding of my career demands and time needed for the business.

What advice do you have for someone contemplating a career in gerontology? In a professional position similar to your current position?

Observe professionals at work in their given field and survey what they find rewarding about work with or related to older adults. Optometrists who sub-specialize in geriatrics or low vision rehabilitation will find their daily job easier as there are so many older adults they are caring for anyway. Having a geriatric-friendly optometry office will simply grow your practice and ensure a high level of proficiency to limit malpractice.

Gerontological Nurse (ADN) Gerontological Nurse (BSN) Gerontological Nurse Practitioner (GNP) Clinical Nurse Specialist in Gerontological Nursing (CNS)

Basic Description: The American Nursing Association (ANA) and the American Nurses Credentialing Center recognize four levels of gerontological nursing certification. **Gerontology Nurses (ADN and BSN)** work directly with older patients in a variety of clinical settings. Using their gerontological training and nursing care skills, they assess direct care needs and situations; manage and implement medications, treatments, and other health care services ordered by other health care professionals; and participate in evaluating the effectiveness of these services. Whenever possible, they involve their elderly patients, family members and caregivers, and others in the processes of care. **Gerontological Nurse Practitioners (GNPs)** have advanced knowledge, clinical skills, and certification that allows them to provide a full range of health care services related to wellness and illness for older patients. They have the training and authority to make differential diagnoses; manage acute and chronic diseases; carry out evidence-based practice; participate in the conduct of research studies; consult with others, including family caregivers, in the care and support network of older patients; and serve as case managers for their patients. They also provide leadership for nursing and other staff members in their work setting and within the nursing profession. They are nursing educators and participate in health policy development and implementation. GNPs are authorized to prescribe medications and treatments in most states. **Clinical Nurse Specialists in Gerontological Nursing (CNSs)** have advanced clinical skills that allow them to provide primary care to older patients, independently or as members of interdisciplinary health care teams, and to serve as resource persons for other staff members in their care of elderly patients. They consult with and guide family caregivers and significant others in the patient's social support network, serve as leaders and supervisors in their work settings, conduct staff and patient education, and are authorized (in some states) to order diagnostic and lab tests, treatments, and medications.

Education and Experience Requirements: An Associate's degree in Nursing (ADN) or Bachelor's degree in Nursing (BSN) is required for certification as a gerontological nurse and a Master's degree (MSN) in Nursing is required for certification as a gerontological nurse practitioner or clinical nurse specialist in gerontological nursing. An MSN is the minimum requirement for serving on the faculty in a registered nurse (RN) and ADN degree programs and a Doctor of Nursing (DSN) or a Doctor of Nursing Practice (DPN) is the minimum requirement for serving on the faculty in BSN, MSN, DPN, and DSN degree programs.

Certification, Licensure, and Continuing Education Requirements: A current, active, unrestricted professional RN license issued by the state or jurisdiction in which the practice occurs is required to practice nursing in the United States. The American Nurses Credentialing Center (ANCC) certifies nurses who practice gerontological nursing at four levels: gerontological nurse (ADN), gerontological nurse (BSN), gerontological nurse practitioner (GNP), and clinical nurse specialist in gerontological nursing (CNS). Eligibility criteria vary for these certificates, but all require RN licensure, specified level(s) of nursing education and amounts of clinical practice, successful completion of the computer-based test (CBT) specific to the certificate being sought, and advanced degree work or continuing education.

Core Competencies and Skills Needed: Core competencies and skills are specified by each type of nursing degree and each level of gerontological nursing certification. Other necessary characteristics include:
- Commitment to patient-centered care and evidence-based practice
- Good communication skills (oral, written, listening)
- Good interpersonal skills
- Good organizational skills

Compensation: This varies by one's education, licensure, experience, level of certification, type of position, employment setting, and the geographic location.

Workplace(s): These include ambulatory care settings (e.g., primary care practices, assisted living facilities, retirement communities, hospice); hospitals and long-term care facilities; settings specific to administration, leadership and public policy (e.g., directors of nursing and vice presidents for nursing in managed care companies, automated medical records companies, state and federal departments, agencies, or organizations); schools of nursing and clinical supervision settings for nursing students; and research centers and institutes.

Employment Outlook: Excellent—demand is greater than supply for all levels of gerontological nurses, including gerontological nurse educators.

Related Professional Organizations and Web Sites:
- American Nursing Association (ANA): www.ana.org
- National Gerontological Nursing Association (NGNA): www.ngna.org
- American Academy of Nursing (AAN): www.aannet.org
- American Nurses Credentialing Center (CANCC): www.nursecredentialing. org
- GeroNurseOnline.org: www.geronurseonline.org
- Building Academic Geriatric Nursing Capacity (BAGNC): www.geriatricnursing. org
- Formal Interest Group on Nursing Care of Older Adults, Gerontological Society of America (GSA): www.geron.org

Grant Writer

Basic Description: Grant writers in gerontology-specific and related settings work with grants for research studies, program development and evaluation, basic program operation, staffing and staff development, and for special projects. They write grants for pilot projects, as well as for the continuation and expansion of existing projects. For each type of grant, however, they essentially carry out the same tasks for each proposal and are involved in the total process from start to finish. They identify and do research on government, foundation, corporate, and other sources of funding; work with program/agency staff to determine the goals and objectives of funding needs; alert staff members of requests for proposals (RFPs) that are relevant to the program or agency's funding needs; write and edit grant proposals and grant-related reports; maintain a calendar for submission and report deadlines; coordinate the preparation and assembly of completed proposals, facilitate delivery of proposals, and track the status of proposal documents; and keep program/agency administrators and other staff apprised of the grant preparation and funding process.

Education and Experience Requirements: A bachelor's degree or higher (master's degree preferred) in a field directly related to the nature and mission of the employing agency, organization, or facility is required. Coursework and/or training workshops in grantsmanship and grant writing are strongly recommended and may be required. Gerontology coursework or a degree component is strongly recommended. Two or more years of professional practice in a related field and evidence of successful grant writing in a related setting may be requested.

Certification, Licensure, and Continuing Education Requirements: Grant writers must meet the requirements of the employing agency, organization, or facility.

Core Competencies and Skills Needed:
- Thorough understanding of the grantsmanship process
- Strong communication skills (written and oral)
- Detail oriented
- Ability to follow directions
- Ability to meet deadlines
- Strong organizational skills
- Ability to multitask
- Knowledge of computer software and relevant databases
- Must enjoy a creative and fast-paced environment
- Ability to work with others from diverse backgrounds

Compensation: This varies by one's education, experience, level of responsibility, and the nature of the employment setting. Some positions may be part-time or on a fee-for-service basis.

Workplace(s): These include community-based organizations and agencies that serve older adults (e.g., senior centers, adult day programs, assisted living, long-term care facilities); aging network agencies (e.g., county commissions, departments, divisions, bureaus on aging; Area Agencies on Aging; Retired Senior Volunteer Programs); adult education and older learner programs.

Employment Outlook: Very good—for experienced grant writers who have demonstrated success at securing funding from a variety of fund-granting sources. An improvement in employment outlook is anticipated for grant writers as more organizations, agencies, and facilities look for funding from new sources to meet the interests and needs of the expanding older adult population.

Related Professional Organizations and Web Sites:
- The Grantsmanship Center: www.tgci.com
- Association for Fundraising Professionals (AFP): www.afpnet.org

Home Care Agency Administrator

Basic Description: The Administrator of a home care agency or in-home assistance program for elders is responsible for overall administration of the agency/program and oversees the day-to-day operation. Job functions include: creating and upholding the organization's vision and values, and leading by example; identifying key goals and objectives, then planning tangible steps for achieving them; personnel recruitment, scheduling, supervision, compensation, coaching, and evaluation; monitoring expenses, developing and monitoring the agency's budget; complying with relevant policies, regulations, and procedures; marketing and public relations; responding to inquiries about agency services; networking with relevant community resources and organizations; assessing client needs and assuring quality care for clients; and dealing with worker compensation, insurance, bonding, and union negotiations.

Education and Experience Requirements: Administrators require a master's degree in gerontological studies, health care administration, social work, nursing, or a closely related field, with gerontology coursework or a degree component in non-gerontology fields. Prior experience in working with older adults is strongly recommended.

Certification, Licensure, and Continuing Education Requirements: Administrators must meet licensure and other requirements mandated by the state in which their professional practice occurs and by the employing agency. Recommended licenses/certificates for this profession include nursing home administrator licensure, home care manager certification, social worker licensure, and registered nurse, or licensed visiting nurse designation. Yearly continuing education is strongly recommended and may be mandated by the licensing authorities and employing agency.

Core Competencies and Skills Needed:
- Updated knowledge of local, state, and federal aging issues and legislation
- Working knowledge of policies and regulations that govern delivery of services for older adults and home care agencies
- Strong communication and interpersonal skills; excellent listener
- Agency and staff management and leadership skills
- Good marketing, public relations, and outreach skills

- Ability to multitask
- Ability to stay calm, patient, and understanding in difficult situations
- Ability to handle difficult and challenging situations

Compensation: This varies by one's education, experience, the nature of the employment setting, and the geographical location.

Workplace(s): These are usually community-based home care agencies.

Employment Outlook: Very Good—due to the increasing number of elders living in the community rather than in care facilities and to the anticipated growth of the older adult population over the next few decades.

Related Professional Organizations and Web Sites:

- American Association for Home Care and Hospice (NAHC): www.nahc. org
- American Association for Homecare (AAHomecare): www.aahomecare.org

An Interview with Quanhong Qiu, Home Care Agency Executive Director

What is your educational background in gerontology and other disciplines or professional fields? What formal credentials (e.g., completed degrees, certification) do you hold in these fields?

My educational background includes a Master's degree in Gerontological Studies, a Master's degree in Management Science and Engineering, and an undergraduate degree in English and International Studies. I also am a Licensed Nursing Home Administrator in the state of Ohio and have a Home Care Manager Certificate granted by the California Association for Health Services at Home (CAHSAH). In addition, I have completed certificates on dementia care updates and other continuing education related to my work.

Briefly describe your gerontology-related career path.

I started to intern as an administer-in-training at an Asian community nursing home in 2001. Then I helped to start a home care agency from scratch after I finished my graduate school. I've been active in educating the community regarding the issues related with aging. As one of the panelists, I gave presentations regarding cultural diversity in health care and end of life care. I was interviewed on radio talks regarding home care with my colleague. I also gave several presentations on how to choose home care, when home care is needed, and other related issues. I came up with the idea of having a Community Health Fair a few years ago. It has been a successful event. It's helpful to educate the community regarding resources available in the community. It was changed to Community Health Festival this year.

How did you first become interested in your current professional position?

The death of my father was kind of a wake up call for me. I realized life is short. While I couldn't do anything for my dad, I wanted to do something that could help other old people. I'd like to make some positive impact in this field. Being an executive director, I have the authority to do mostly what I think are the right things to do. I prefer to help people stay in their homes rather than go to care facilities.

What are the most rewarding aspects of your career?

Knowing that we're helping people and helping to better the quality of life of our clients are the most rewarding aspects of my career.

What are the most challenging aspects of your career?

The most challenging aspects of my career are: the difficulty of recruiting and retaining enough good quality caregivers, difficult clients, pressure to continuously grow business with the fierce competition, and clients who are not willingly to spend money in home care or can't afford to pay it privately.

Describe a typical workday in your current professional position.

Update meeting with staff; problem-solving, coaching, counseling staff and clients as needed; make plans for the day, week, and month; outreach and public relations; budgeting, looking into the financial statements to ensure the accuracy, and promptly following up on collecting payments from clients; help with intake of new clients, inquiries, assessments, in-service training, and staffing as needed; and communicate with corporate managers and other personnel (i.e., report to corporate; follow instructions from corporate personnel, and request necessary changes, clarification, and other assistance) as needed.

How do you balance career and other aspects of your life?

I make sure to take time to relax and to spend time with my husband when I'm off duty. I integrate spirituality into my daily life. I like dancing, swimming, hiking, and travel. It helps to improve myself, keep myself calm, do the right things, and make right decisions.

What advice do you have for someone contemplating a career in gerontology? In a professional position similar to your current position?

Ask yourself twice if working with older adults is really a career that you want. It's a career that needs someone who has passion about this field. If you work for a start-up company or agency, be prepared that you probably have to put lots of time and effort into it. There could be ups and downs. Persistence, perseverance, positive attitude, staying calm, being flexible, and focusing on what's important will be helpful in the position. There could be more time, money and effort needed than you thought to provide high quality services.

Horticultural Therapist

Basic Description: Horticultural therapists are trained to use gardening as a therapeutic tool to help their clients and patients achieve treatment-specific goals. They involve those with whom they work in all phases of gardening, from plant selection and propagation to the final use of the garden products, as a means of providing cognitive therapy, social growth, physical rehabilitation, and/or vocational training. Horticultural therapists commonly work as members of multidisciplinary rehabilitation teams (along with doctors, psychiatrists, psychologists, social workers, counselors, occupational therapists, physical therapists and/or medical or human service professionals).

Education and Experience Requirements: A minimum of a bachelor's degree in horticultural therapy or an equivalent horticultural therapy bachelor's degree that includes horticultural science courses (40 semester hours), horticultural therapy specialization courses (8 semester hours), therapy/human science courses (24 semester hours), and a horticultural therapy internship (1,000 clock hours) supervised by a registered horticultural therapist (HTR or HTM) is required. Gerontology coursework or a degree component is recommended for those who plan to work with elders.

Certification, Licensure, and Continuing Education Requirements: The Horticultural Therapist Registered (HTR) certification requires the American Horticultural Therapy Association (AHTA)-specified bachelor's degree. HTR candidates must earn a total of four AHTA points, including at least 2,000 hours of paid employment in horticultural therapy. AHTA points may also be accumulated through AHTA-approved activities, such as continuing education, workshop presentations or coordination, direct service to AHTA, and publications.

Core Competencies and Skills Needed:
- Ability to create barrier-free garden spaces to accommodate clients/patients with a wide range of abilities
- Comfortable working with clients who are physically, mentally, and/or socially disabled
- Ability to work collaboratively as a member of a rehabilitation team

- Enjoy gardening; comfortable with getting your hands dirty and working outside
- Patience

Compensation: This varies by one's educational background, HTR certification, type of practice, the nature of the workplace, amount of experience, and the geographical location.

Workplace(s): These include rehabilitation centers, psychiatric and mental health clinics, hospitals and medical centers, hospice, correctional facilities, long-term care and assisted living centers, senior centers, community and botanical gardens, and occupational training facilities and programs.

Employment Outlook: Good;—especially as HTR certification gains recognition as a valid professional credential.

Related Professional Organizations and Web Sites:
- American Horticultural Therapy Association (AHTA): www.ahta.org

Human Factors Engineer Ergonomist Gerontechnologist

Basic Description: Human factors/ergonomics is an applied, multidisciplinary field of study and practice that is concerned with the interactions and fit between humans and other system elements to optimize performance and well-being for humans and for overall system performance. When an older adult is the human in the system, the goal is to find an optimal fit between the demand or desire to function and the ability to function at a level adequate to meet the demand or desire. The work of human factors engineers, ergonomists, and gerontechnologists (although these position titles are used synonymously, there appear to be some unique aspects of each that are not yet clearly defined by professionals in these fields) is based in a systems approach that is user-centered. As researchers with gerontology interests, they seek to understand the impact of age-related changes on the daily task and activity performance of elders; identify human, environmental, and product problems and difficulties that affect task and activity performance; and discover solutions to these problems and difficulties. As designers, they may create new products or redesign existing products; modify environments; develop intervention strategies; or provide training to change personal or staff behaviors that prevent or limit optimal performance for older persons. For example, this approach is being applied to elders' living and work environments (e.g., fall prevention, workplace ergonomics), mobility and transportation (e.g., vehicle design, modification of roadway signage, traffic lights), and use of technology in everyday life (e.g., interactive communication systems, monitoring devices, entertainment devices such as TVs, VCRs/DVDs, and videogames).

Education and Experience Requirements: A master's or doctoral degree in human factors engineering/ergonomics, industrial engineering, computer science, biomedical engineering, psychology-behavioral sciences, industrial/organizational psychology, applied experimental psychology, aviation human factors, occupational safety and ergonomics, environmental health and safety, human-machine systems engineering, or other technology-related fields is required. Gerontology coursework or a degree component is strongly encouraged.

Certification, Licensure, and Continuing Education Requirements: Professionals must meet requirements specified by their professional field, employer, and/or the state(s) in which their practice occurs.

Core Competencies and Skills Needed:
- Ability to work cooperatively and collaboratively
- Creative and innovative approach to problem-solving
- Competence in use of assessment methods and skills
- Competence in research methodologies and statistical analyses
- Commitment to a user-centered approach
- Good understanding of changes in human function with age
- Technology literacy

Compensation: This varies according to professional position, the nature of the workplace, one's educational background, and experience.

Workplace(s): These include institutions of higher education, research units in industry, and government organizations.

Employment Outlook: Promising—but still to be determined for this emerging and multidisciplinary field.

Related Professional Organizations and Web Sites:
- Human Factors and Ergonomics Society (HFES): www.hfes.org
- HFES Aging Technical Group (ATG): www.psychology.gatech.edu/atg/

- Center for Research and Education on Aging and Technology Enhancement (CREATE): www.psychology.gatech.edu/create/
- International Ergonomics Association (IEA): www.iea.cc/
- International Society of Gerontechnology (ISG): www.gerontechnology.info

In-Home Services Program Director, County Commission on Aging

Basic Description: The In-Home Services Program Director for a county commission on aging (COA) administers the day-to-day operation of in-home services, such as case management, homemaking, personal care, respite care, caregiver training, prescription drug assistance and emergency need, chore services, and related supplemental programs for persons 60 years of age and older who reside within the COA service area and need in-home services to maintain independence. The Director is responsible for the preparation of program grant proposals; oversight of grant-funded program delivery; evaluation of grant project effectiveness; development of program budgets and maintenance of budget-related records; recruitment, training, supervision, evaluation, and discipline of in-home services' full-time staff members and part-time contract workers; preparation of monthly financial reports and quarterly program reports; annual program reviews; networking with local, regional, and state agencies within the aging network; speaking publicly on behalf of the commission; liaison with and membership on boards and committees of local and state organizations, including institutions of higher education in the COA service area; and, when applicable, supervision of social work interns from local colleges/universities.

Education and Experience Requirements: A Bachelor's (BSW) or Master's (MSW) degree in Social Work from a program accredited by the Council of Social Work Education (CWSE) is required (MSW is preferred). Also required is at least 7–10 years of experience in an aging services program and 5–7 years of supervision experience. Gerontology coursework or a degree component strongly recommended.

Certification, Licensure, and Continuing Education Requirements: Directors must meet the requirements for licensure in the state where the professional practice occurs and the continuing education required for licensure by the employing agency.

Core Competencies and Skills Needed:
- Good working knowledge of aging processes and aging issues
- Personnel supervision and administration skills
- Strong interpersonal skills
- Strong communication skills (oral, written, and listening)
- Commitment to client-centered professional practice
- Good working knowledge of needs assessment tools and processes
- Public speaking skills
- Good working knowledge of board/committee processes
- Good organizational skills
- Good financial and personnel record-keeping skills

Compensation: This varies by one's education, experience, and geographical location.

Workplace(s): This is typically the county commission on aging (or similar agency), which is usually located in the county seat (or in the largest county seat if two or more counties are involved).

Employment Outlook: Good.

Related Professional Organizations and Web Sites:
- National Association of Social Workers (NASW): www.socialworkers.org
- American Society on Aging (ASA): www.asaging.org
- National Council on Aging (NCOA): www.ncoa.org
- State Offices or Departments on Aging

An Interview with
Barbara Slack Frankenfield,
In-Home Services Program
Director, County Commission
on Aging

What is your educational background in gerontology and other disciplines or professional fields? What formal credentials (e.g., completed degrees, certification) do you hold in these fields?

I hold a Bachelor's of Science in Social Welfare. I am licensed in the state of Michigan as a social worker.

Briefly describe your gerontology-related career path.

Like many other social workers, I believed that I wanted to spend my professional career working with children. I liked the gerontology-related courses during my academic career but did not feel a strong urge to work with older adults. After three months of job search, I was offered a job as a case manager working with older adults in a community action agency. Given that this was my first and only opportunity to work in the field in which I was trained, I decided to take the job and continue to search for something that would allow me to work with children. After about three months, however, I realized that working in the field of aging was exactly where I wanted to be. After 16 months with the community action agency, I accepted a position as the supervisor of the Senior Companion Program (SCP) in Columbus, Ohio. This program was new to Columbus, so I was fortunate to assist with the development of the program. Five years later, and after a move to Michigan, I spent two years as a hospital social worker, working primarily with older adults. For the past 23 years, I have been the In-Home Services Program Director for a county commission on aging. After 32 years in the field, I consider myself fortunate to be working in a profession that continues to be challenging and life-giving.

How did you first become interested in your current professional position?

When I moved to my current residence in rural Michigan, I knew that I wanted to continue to work in the field of aging. I completed an application at the commission on aging and, hearing that there were no jobs available at the time, began to volunteer in the community. Volunteering gave me an opportunity to get to know the agency and the community.

What are the most rewarding aspects of your career?

My profession has given me the opportunity to meet so many people from so many "walks of life." My life has been enriched by clients/consumers and by coworkers. After 32 years, I continue to be honored that clients have been willing to share their lives with me, usually at a time when they are very vulnerable or in a state of despair or confusion. One of my best friends for the last 23 years is a woman whose birthday is one day before mine but she is forty years older. We had a big celebration when she turned 90 and I turned 50.

What are the most challenging aspects of your career?

My career happens every day at the local level. I know how federal, state, and local policies affect the amount of assistance people are able to receive. I see daily how hard people work to maintain their independence, to provide care for a loved one, to deal with retirement issues, to deal with fading memories. Often, the most challenging aspect of my career is dealing with the political process and the incredible amount of paperwork.

Describe a typical workday in your current professional position.

I'm not sure there is a "typical" workday in a commission on aging. Maybe "typical" could be described by the word "interruptions." Days are filled with financial and program reports, meetings, calls from people who need resources or assistance dealing with Medicare and Medicaid issues, staff issues, scheduling of services for clients, dealing with walk-in clients, keeping up with "news" in the world of gerontology, and networking. Though not typical, days are interesting.

How do you balance career and other aspects of your life?

I am fortunate to have a job I love and coworkers who are supportive and fun. Also, I have a partner who understands the ins and outs of human services and is very supportive. It helps that I have friends from other professions and that I remember to relax and have fun. I also have lots of other interests that take my mind off the professional aspect. I love to read, play my guitar, work in the yard and I am passionate about women's college basketball, which I'm sure bores my friends.

What advice do you have for someone contemplating a career in gerontology? In a professional position similar to your current position?

Go for it!!! It will be challenging, especially with the changing face of aging, and be sure to make it fun. The human services profession can be stressful, so be sure to make time for yourself, have friends who are supportive, and keep a sense of humor.

Intergenerational Specialist

Basic Description: Intergenerational specialists develop, administer, and evaluate programs and services that link older adults and young people in ways that are interactive and mutually beneficial to both age groups.

Education and Experience Requirements: Intergenerational specialists require a minimum of a bachelor's degree in education, human development, or a related field. Having a background in both child and adult development/ gerontology is strongly recommended.

Certification, Licensure, and Continuing Education Requirements: These may be required by the employing agency, organization, or facility and may vary by state.

Core Competencies and Skills Needed:
According to the proposed "standards of intergenerational practice":
* Possess adequate knowledge of human development across the life span to support planning and implementation of intergenerational programs of mutual benefit to both older adult and youth program participants
* Understand the need for and use effective communication skills appropriate to development intergenerational relationships
* Demonstrate commitment to collaboration and partnership in program planning, administration, and evaluation
* Integrate knowledge from a variety of disciplines and fields of study in the development of intergenerational programming
* Employ appropriate evaluation strategies and techniques, adapted from fields such as education and the social sciences, to inform program development for diverse age groups and settings
* Be self-reflective, caring, and true to the intended purpose of intergenerational programming

Others:
* Familiarity with curriculum development and program planning skills
* Grantsmanship and fundraising skills
* Effective oral and written communication skills
* Ability to think creatively and be innovative

Compensation: This varies by the nature of the employing agency, organization, or facility. Compensation may be based on part-time positions paid by wage rather than salary. Some positions may exist only as part of time-limited grant projects.

Workplace(s): These include preschools and K-12 schools, Head Start programs, after-school programs, child care centers, senior centers, intergenerational day care centers, community education or recreation programs/ departments, community arts and theatre programs, libraries, chronic disease-focused organizations, medical centers, long-term care facilities, retirement communities, senior living and Grandfamilies housing, Foster Grandparent Programs (FGPs), multigenerational center, faith-based institutions, and human service agencies that serve both older adults and youth.

Employment Outlook: Excellent—due to new legislation, increasing visibility of intergenerational issues, increasing diversity of employment opportunities, development of professional standards of practice, and K-12 aging education initiatives.

Related Professional Organizations and Web Sites:
- Generations United: www.gu.org
- Center for Intergenerational Learning at Temple University: http://templecil. org
- *Journal of Intergenerational Relationships* published by Haworth Press: www. HaworthPress.com

---

Interior Designer-Gerontology Specialization Healthcare Interior Designer

Basic Description: Interior designers work with clients to design interior spaces that meet their client's aesthetic, functional, and safety needs. "Person-environment fit" is a key concept for interior designers, regardless of the specific nature of their professional practice. While many design living spaces, others design the materials and products, such as the fabrics, furniture, lighting, household appliances, and accessories. **Interior Designers-Gerontology Specialization** design or redesign spaces for older persons in private residences (e.g., individual houses, apartments, condominiums), age-segregated residences and communities (e.g., retirement living centers); and age-integrated residences/communities (e.g., intergenerational Grandfamilies housing). Interior designers working to maintain elders in their own homes incorporate the concept of "aging in place." Some work with elders who are relocating to smaller residential settings and care facilities or help to retrofit existing living spaces to accommodate the changing physical, mental, and/or social needs of the individual residents or family unit. **Healthcare Interior Designers** are more likely to work with developers, architects, corporate administrators and planners, and construction managers in planning new healthcare and "senior living" facilities from the ground up.

Education and Experience Requirements: A minimum of a bachelor's degree in interior design from a program accredited by the Council for Interior Design Accreditation is required. Gerontology coursework or a degree component strongly recommended.

Certification, Licensure, and Continuing Education Requirements: The National Council for Interior Design Qualification (NCIDQ) certification is based on examination and portfolio review, after the education and experience requirements have been met. The American Academy of Healthcare Interior Designers (AAHID) certification is strongly recommended upon completion of education and experience requirements for those who wish to specialize in healthcare interior design. Maintaining AAHID certification requires a specified number continuing education credits each year. Certification as an aging-in-place specialist, which is granted through the National Association of Home Builders (NAHB) University of Housing, is available to interior designers.

Core Competencies and Skills Needed:
- Interest in physical spaces
- Is creative, imaginative, and artistic
- Good organizational skills
- Ability to self-discipline
- Good interpersonal skills; comfortable working with diverse professionals and clients
- Good written and oral communication skills
- Attentive listener
- Interest in technical thinking and problem-solving
- Good negotiation and mediation skills
- Good working knowledge of codes and regulations that govern interior design
- Good working knowledge of materials and products used for interior design purposes

- Ability to be both a team leader and a team player
- Excellent time and project management abilities
- Understanding of business planning
- Understanding of changing needs of elders due to normal aging, changes in physical and/or mental health conditions, and changes in social and economic factors

Compensation: This varies by one's educational background, experience, type of certification, quality of performance, the nature of the employment setting, focus of professional practice, and geographical location.

Workplace(s): These include interior design firms, architectural firms, manufacturing firms (e.g., manufacturers of furniture, fabrics, wall coverings, and related products), healthcare and "senior living" corporations, independent consulting, and sole proprietor practices.

Employment Outlook: Limited—but promising for these emerging interior design specializations, especially in regard to healthcare and "senior living" communities and facilities.

Related Professional Organizations and Web Sites:
- Council for Interior Design Accreditation (CIDA): http://www.accredit-id.org
- National Council for Interior Design Qualification (NCIDQ): http://www.ncidq.org
- American Academy of Healthcare Interior Designers (AAHID): http://aahid.org
- American Society of Interior Design (ASID): www. asid.org
- Interior Design Educators Council (IDEC): www.idec.org
- Careers in Interior Design: www.careersininteriordesign.com
- National Aging in Place Council (NAIPC): www.naipc.org
- National Association of Home Builders (NAHB): www.nahb.org
- Formal Interest Group on Physical Environments and Aging, Gerontological Society of America (GSA): www.geron.org

An Interview with
Jane F. Dailey,
Healthcare Interior Designer

What is your educational background in gerontology and other disciplines or professional fields? What formal credentials (e.g., completed degrees, certification) do you hold in these fields?

I earned a Bachelor of Science degree in Finance in 1980 and a Bachelor of Arts degree in Interior Design in 1992. I have completed all but the thesis for a Master's degree in Interior Design and Gerontology. I am certified by both the National Council for Interior Design Qualification (NCIDQ) and the American Academy of Healthcare Interior Designers (AAHID).

Briefly describe your gerontology-related career path.

Upon completion of my interior design BA degree I had the opportunity to work for an interior design firm that specialized in healthcare design. This area of design is probably the most technical of all areas because life safety codes are always first priority. I found this to be both interesting and challenging. I was offered a graduate assistantship at the University of Akron and had the opportunity to gobble up many additional credits. I decided to focus my interest in healthcare design and found gerontology to be my most beloved path. After graduate school, I was fortunate to work for an architectural firm that specialized in design for aging. This firm not only had vast experience in the field, but also had great passion for it. Later, I made the decision to go into consulting and work directly for the senior living communities in northeast Ohio.

How did you first become interested in your current professional position?

When I decided to go to graduate school, I was having a conversation with a friend who also happened to be a career counselor. I knew I was interested in healthcare design and I knew that as a graduate assistant I would have more credits available to me than I actually needed for my interior design degree. What to do? My friend suggested "Gerontology." I said, "What's that?" He said, "The study of aging." I thought it sounded like a pretty smart idea, especially with the baby boomers on the way up. This started me on my gerontology coursework, however, I quickly found out that not only was it a good idea, it was my PASSION! I loved this path. I think the long and short of it for me is: Gerontology is not what I do or what I study. It is who I am; it goes to my core.

What are the most rewarding aspects of your career?

I love the residents. I learn so much from them and always enjoy my interactions with them. I am thrilled when they are happy with the changes in their "house." I am rewarded when I include some crazy new idea (evidence-based, of course) and it really does some good. This has been an incredibly satisfying career for me.

What are the most challenging aspects of your career?

Most definitely, the greatest challenges come from the residents. They are cautious of change and often see no need for it (for example, "The carpet is perfectly good, we don't need to spend the money."). They always have strong opinions and will always express them. Getting consensus can be tough some days, however, I try always to include the residents in the design process (providing the community will allow it). After all, it's their house, not mine.

Describe a typical workday in your current professional position.

The "typical" workday doesn't really exist since there are so many aspects to a project. The design process begins with the first client meeting. What are they hoping to accomplish? What are the needs? What can we realistically do within the confines of the budget? Then there is the period of design development, when the ideas begin to take shape. The process moves forward and the design gradually is refined. At last, the construction begins. Most projects take many months; some take several years. There is constant client interaction—meetings, presentations, and questions. Then, of course, there are always fires that need to be put out! Outside of client meetings, there are meetings with sales reps. In order to do the best possible work, a designer must always keep current on available resources. Finally, there are conferences and educational opportunities. This specialty is young and constantly evolving. New research comes out regularly and the designer must stay on top of it.

How do you balance career and other aspects of your life?

I work 40 hours a week—not 50 or 60. When I go home, I leave my work in the office. My family always comes first. I was fortunate to work for employers who shared these views. Any way you do it, however, it is a balancing act.

What advice do you have for someone contemplating a career in gerontology? In a professional position similar to your current position?

My advice for anyone considering a career in gerontology would be this: If you enjoy spending time with old people, then this may be the place for you. If not, you may want to consider another path. It's not really as simple as it sounds. People who work in gerontology are passionate about what they do and they do it because they really love elders. For those who would like to pursue a career in design, I would first advise that they look for an interior design program that is accredited by the Council for Interior Design Accreditation. Generally, the best programs come out of the schools of architecture, but this is not always true. Some still come out of the schools of family and consumer sciences. It is also important to have good drawing skills and a good program will teach you this. Take as many gerontology courses as you can. Finally, the best teacher is always experience.

K-12 Teacher
K-12 Curriculum Developer
K-12 Curriculum Specialist
on Aging

Basic Description: Over the past decade, an increasing amount of attention has been paid to the development of aging education for elementary and secondary school students. Three primary avenues for integration of aging education into the K-12 curriculum have been the development of: curriculum standards on aging in subject matter areas (e.g., social studies, health, and language arts); curricula, courses, activities and materials on aging for grades K-12; and intergenerational service learning opportunities for K-12 students. The goal is to infuse aging education into the curriculum of existing subject matter areas rather than creating a new subject matter area. Leadership for these initiatives has been provided by the National Academy for Teaching and Learning about Aging (NATLA) at the University of North Texas, the Institute of Gerontology at Ithaca College, and the Association for Gerontology in Higher Education's K-12 Task Force. Also, some state vocational education departments have added career path training in adult care services for vocational students at the secondary school level. To date, however, teacher training on aging has primarily been through in-service training, summer institutes, and access to online resources. While many pre-service teacher education students have access to gerontology courses and degree components (e.g., an undergraduate minor in gerontology), such coursework must be added to their teacher training program rather than being an integral part of it. Regardless, three new career path options that combine teaching and aging education are beginning to emerge: **K-12 Teachers** who infuse aging education into their subject matter curricula; **K-12 Curriculum Developers** are teachers who are selected by organizations such as NATLA to become aging education curriculum developers for specific grades at the elementary school level; and **K-12 Curriculum Specialists on Aging** are experienced master teachers who earn graduate degrees with a gerontology focus or degree component and then move into curriculum specialist positions at the district level, in state departments of education, and in teacher education departments or gerontology centers/institutes in higher education.

Education and Experience Requirements: A minimum of a bachelor's degree in elementary or secondary education with gerontology coursework or degree component is required. A master's or doctoral degree is required for curriculum specialist positions.

Certification, Licensure, and Continuing Education Requirements: Individuals must meet state requirements for teacher certification and continuing education requirements to renew certification.

Core Competencies and Skills Needed:
- Working knowledge of curriculum infusion methodologies
- Understanding of how aging connects to core subject matter
- Creativity and innovation in designing learning strategies and experiences
- Ability to evaluate textbook and teaching material content on aging
- Understanding of the diversity among older persons and of the experience of aging

Compensation: This varies by one's education, experience, the nature of the employment setting, the level of responsibility, and the geographical location.

Workplace(s): These include K-12 schools and school-based intergenerational programs; school district and intermediate school district offices, state departments of education, teacher education departments; and gerontology programs, centers, or institutes at colleges and universities.

Employment Outlook: Limited—but with potential for growth.

Related Professional Organizations and Web Sites:
- National Academy for Teaching and Learning about Aging (NATLA): www.cps.unt.edu/natla
- Association for Gerontology in Higher Education (AGHE), K-12 Task Force: www.aghe.org
- Ithaca College Institute for Gerontology, Lesson Plans on Aging Issues Project: www.ithaca.edu/aging/schools

Life Event Services Manager
Life Event Specialist

Basic Description: Life Event Services Managers assist the firm's financial advisors and clients through the delivery of information and expertise related to healthcare, long-term care, Social Security, estate planning, taxes, education planning, and caregiving for aging relatives or other family-related financial issues. Responsibilities include the creation of a vision and strategy; development of training materials for financial advisors; hiring of associates; implementation of a firm-wide internal marketing strategy; management of vendor relationships and high service standards; development and maintenance of an easily navigable internal Web site; improvement of the current financial planning process; ensuring that the subject matter experts remain current in their area(s) of expertise; working closely with other product areas; educating and training the financial advisors; making presentations at financial advising conferences/seminars; and working with all channels to ensure consistency of message. **Life Event Specialists** are responsible for positioning the financial advisors as valued and trusted professionals who work with clients in transition to later life and family caregiving roles. They also work with the firm's financial advisors and clients to discuss specific situations and offer education, practical solutions, and advice; assist in the creation and marketing of gerontology-related topical publications for both internal and external use; and train the financial advisors through conferences, seminars, and computer-based approaches.

Educational and Experience Requirements: Life Event Services Managers require a master's or doctoral degree in gerontology or a closely related profession, with gerontology coursework or a degree component for non-gerontology degrees. Eight-plus years of experience in social work, aging and the retirement process, product marketing, product development, financial planning, and the needs of affluent investors or related activities is also required. **Life Event Specialists** require a bachelor's degree in social work, sociology, applied sociology, finance, or a closely related field. Designation as a Registered Health Underwriter (RHU) and FTCP (or equivalents) or an advanced degree in gerontology is strongly encouraged. Five or more years of experience in social services, healthcare services, or education with a focus in gerontology and issues related to Medicare and Social Security is required.

Certification, Licensure, and Continuing Education Requirements: These professionals must meet requirements mandated by the state where their professional practice occurs and by their employing firm.

Core Competencies and Skills Needed:

Life Event Services Manager:

* Must be a self-starter
* Excellent interpersonal, verbal/written communication and public speaking skills
* Proven track record in developing business relationships
* Management/leadership skills

Life Event Specialist:

* Direct training and presentation skills
* Proficient in Microsoft Office
* Must be able to travel overnight

Compensation: This varies by one's education, experience, type and level of position within the firm, the nature of the employment setting, and the geographical location.

Workplace(s): These include banks, bank holding companies, and full-service brokerage firms.

Employment Outlook: Promising—but as yet undetermined for these newly emerging career positions.

Related Professional Organizations and Web Sites: None have been identified yet.

Marriage and Family Therapist (MFT)

Basic Description: Marriage and Family Therapists (MFTs) are mental health professionals who use a holistic, psychotherapeutic, and family systems approach in their professional practice. The family, rather than an individual, is the unit of practice and this often means inclusion of family members from two or more generations of a family. Marriage and family therapy is intentionally short-term, problem-centered, and solution-focused. The intent of therapy is to move the family unit toward solution of the problem on which the therapy is focused, as effectively, efficiently, and quickly as possible. Problems addressed by MFTs include marital distress; child or adolescent behaviors; inter- and multigenerational conflicts; problems related to eating disorders, alcoholism, and drug abuse; chronic conditions, such as depression, schizophrenia, autism, affective (mood) disorders, and other mental health conditions; chronic physical illnesses; family violence; and sexual abuse. Less visible, but emerging, is marriage and family therapy practice with older adults and their families, in which the focus is on problems centered around or more related to the family elders. This includes concerns, issues, and problems related to custodial grandparenting and kinship care, grandparent visitation rights, widowhood, divorce of older couples, remarriage in later life, adult stepfamilies, caregiving for family elders, death of elderly parents, and inheritance. MFTs with doctoral degrees may become college/university faculty members or administrators in college and university departments of counseling and guidance, family studies/family science, or marriage and family therapy.

Education and Experience Requirements: A master's or doctoral degree in marriage and family therapy from a program accredited by the Commission on Accreditation for Marriage and Family Therapy Education (COAMFTE) or a master's or doctoral degree in a related mental health field (such as psychiatry, clinical psychology, clinical social work, counseling, education), followed by a postgraduate COAMFTE-accredited clinical training program in marriage and family therapy is required. Gerontology coursework or a degree component is strongly recommended for those who plan to treat family system problems of elders and their families. A doctorate that includes research training and experience is required for college/university teaching, research, and administrative positions.

Certification, Licensure, and Continuing Education Requirements: Licensure or certification is required to practice in most states. Eligibility for licensure includes completion of an extensive (approximately 2 years) post-graduate supervised clinical experience and sitting for either the state licensing examination or the MFT national examination conducted by the Association of Marriage and Family Therapy Regulatory Boards (AMFTRB).

Core Competencies and Skills Needed:
* Excellent interpersonal skills; demonstrated success in working with individuals and groups
* Emotional maturity
* Excellent verbal communication and attentive listening skills
* Patience
* Committed to a client-centered (rather than therapist-centered) approach to practice
* Creativity and resourcefulness

Compensation: This varies by one's education, experience, type of practice, and the nature of the employment setting.

Workplace(s): These include private practices, in-patient physical and mental health facilities, courts and prisons, community health centers, social service agencies, community-based agencies and organizations that serve elders, shelters for homeless persons or victims of domestic violence, and college/university-based academic departments, counseling centers, and research institutes.

Employment Outlook: Excellent—especially with growth in the elderly population, the expanding scope of marriage and family therapy practice, and an aging population that is more comfortable engaging in therapeutic processes.

Related Professional Organizations and Web Sites:
* American Association of Marriage and Family Therapy (AAMFT): www.aamft.org
* National Council on Family Relations (NCFR): www.ncfr.org

Mediator
Family Mediator
Elder Care Mediator

Basic Description: Alternative Dispute Resolution (ADR) grew out of the need for identifying ways to resolve conflicts other than by taking a dispute into the courts or resorting to violence. ADR is also known by the more common terms of conflict resolution and mediation. In part, the popularity of mediation is due to the fact that it is a confidential and voluntary process in which a neutral third party mediator facilitates civil discussion of the problems at issue and works with the disputing parties as they negotiate an equitable resolution. Mediation, negotiation, and arbitration are the most common forms of ADR. Mediation is the type of conflict resolution service most frequently requested in family dispute situations. Other forms of dispute/conflict resolution include: combined mediation-arbitration, early neutral evaluation, community conferencing, collaborative law, negotiated rulemaking, and peer mediation. Mediators who work with family conflict resolution are known as family mediators, and they deal with a wide variety of family conflict issues, including: prenuptial agreements, divorce, custody issues, adoption, parent-child and sibling-sibling relationship problems, family business concerns, property division, inheritance, and conflicts with neighbors or among friends. Divorce mediation originally created the need for family mediation services and remains the most frequently used form for family disputes. Recently, however, the use of mediation has increased considerably for conflicts related to the care of elders and kinship care (when grandparents or other relatives provide primary care for related children/grandchildren under the age of 18 years). Mediation is also a productive process for use in situations related to employment and retirement for older adults, in situations related to the housing of elders, and provision of in-home or institutional care for elders.

Education and Experience Requirements: Requirements for mediator education, training, and credentialing is handled at the state level. Some states license, register, or certify mediators. Mediation training usually involves 40 hours of basic training, plus 20 hours of advanced training. Some mediators seek further education through a conflict resolution degree or certificate program at institutions of higher education. For family mediators an undergraduate or graduate degree in family studies or marriage and family therapy is strongly encouraged. For mediators who work with elders, gerontology coursework or a degree component would be very helpful. Professionals in the fields of counseling and guidance, social work, law, and clinical psychology who work with families and/or elders should find mediation training to be an excellent addition to their professional "toolkit."

Certification, Licensure, and Continuing Education Requirements: Mediators must meet licensure, certification, or registration requirements of state in which the mediation practice occurs. Continuing education is required by some states for license or registration renewal or for recertification.

Core Competencies and Skills Needed:
- Working knowledge of different models of conflict resolution
- Working knowledge of the process and stages of collaborative problem-solving
- Understanding of the sources of power in negotiation
- Ability to handle issues related to diversity
- Ability to diffuse emotionally-charged disputes
- Ability to mediate and negotiate multiparty disputes
- Ability to draft durable agreements
- Effective communication skills
- Active listening skills

Compensation: This varies by education; type and amount of mediation training and experience; state licensure, registration or certification; the nature of the employment setting, and the geographic location. The range of compensation may include volunteer services, pro bono work, part-time wages, and part-time or full-time salary or fee for service.

Workplace(s): These include community mediation and conflict resolution centers, courts, human service agencies, law firms, state and federal governmental agencies, long-term care and assisted living centers, senior centers and other community-based settings that serve older adults, and private practices or consultancies.

Employment Outlook: Good—with the likelihood of improvement as more elders turn to conflict resolution, including mediation, to resolve family disputes and other conflicts.

Related Professional Organizations and Web Sites:
- Association for Conflict Resolution (ACR): www.acrnet.org
- National Council on Family Relations (NCFR): www.ncfr.org
- American Association of Marriage and Family Therapists (AAMFT): www.aamft.org

An Interview with
Susan J. Butterwick,
Mediator, Mediation Trainer,
and Attorney

What is your educational background in gerontology and other disciplines or professional fields? What formal credentials (e.g., completed degrees, certification) do you hold in these fields?

I have a BFA degree from a university in Michigan and a JD degree from a law school in Ohio. I was trained as a mediator prior to earning my law degree. In law school and in my subsequent law practice, I came to better understand the value of collaborative problem solving, as compared to the court process, particularly on cases involving family matters. I was trained first in basic community mediation and then went on to other advanced mediation trainings, including adult guardianship mediation. Although my education does not include formal training in gerontology, I have learned a lot about working with elderly people and families through directing and researching elder mediation projects, mediating with elders and families in conflict over care issues, working with various service providers in the aging network, and, in my personal life, caring for my 99-year-old father-in-law in our home. Two years ago, I sat on the caregiving content committee for the state Office of Services to the Aging to draft a statewide aging public policy agenda.

Briefly describe your gerontology-related career path.

A research study and a national demonstration project, both with The Center for Social Gerontology (TCSG), were my first gerontology-related professional experiences beyond mediating adult guardianship cases, which I had been doing for several years before directing these projects. The intent of the research study, funded by the State Justice Institute, was to determine the efficacy of adult guardianship mediation programs in four states. Next, I served as the directing attorney for the Caregiver Adult Guardianship Mediation Project (2001–2004). As the sole mediator on the TCSG staff, I was responsible for working with mediators, training, and program policies, as well as performing educational outreach and collaborating with stakeholders for the project. For the past several years, I have worked with a dispute resolution center in a local county on their adult guardianship/caregiver program. I also train mediators in adult guardianship mediation for the State Court Administrative Office and work with dispute resolution centers to develop best practices to make the necessary accommodations in mediating with elderly individuals. As the training director for a dispute resolution center, I am working with the state Long-Term Care Ombudsman's office on a proposal for conflict resolution training for ombudspersons and facility staff members. I continue to gain understanding about the issues that elders and their caregivers face. The people on both sides of the table (the elderly parent and their caregivers or children) who come to mediation struggle with many of the same issues that I see in my every day life.

How did you first become interested in your current professional position?

I was trained as a mediator in 1993, before I received my law degree. As a mediator, I first became interested in working with families. As an attorney, I worked with juvenile cases and quickly realized that there were better places than the courtroom for families to resolve many of their interpersonal differences, which spurred my interest in family mediation. I received specialized training in adult guardianship mediation and then in other specialized areas dealing with families and children. While coordinating a child protection mediation program, I became interested in setting up and evaluating mediation programs serving families. It was a natural progression to work on the adult guardianship mediation program study and, from there, to direct the caregiver/adult guardianship mediation demonstration project.

What are the most rewarding aspects of your career?

The privilege of being able to sit down with families as a neutral person who can listen to them in a different way and help them hear one another, hold everyone's views as valid without having to choose between them or "judge" them, and facilitate their development of their own ideas and solutions to remedy the problems they are facing, is incredibly rewarding and satisfying to me. Regardless of whether I'm performing this service as a volunteer mediator for a community dispute resolution center, as a private practitioner when I mediate court cases, or as a salaried program director, the level of personal satisfaction is the same. I also enjoy training other mediators to do this important work so that these services can expand and grow.

What are the most challenging aspects of your career?

Keeping everything straight with so many balls in the air and refocusing as I move from one task or project to another is a major challenge. (I also direct other family and school mediation projects.) There is no question that it is rewarding to facilitate families in resolving their interpersonal conflicts, but it can also be emotionally draining to see people struggle with very difficult issues (such as family caregiving) for which there is little support and scant resources for them to access. Family cases tend to "stick" with me longer after mediation than other kinds of cases.

Describe a typical workday in your current professional position.

Every day is different, which is another reason I love what I do. I work for several employers on several programs. On some days, I only mediate cases. On other days, I may only teach or train. On other days, I'm working on a program in another city. At other times, I'm writing. I enjoy the combination of working in solitude and of working with people either in mediation or through teaching students and mediators.

How do you balance career and other aspects of your life?

When I'm working by myself, I'm able to work in an office or at home when caregiving responsibilities require me to be there. Putting all the pieces together, however, can be a challenge that I do not always meet as well as I (or others) would like. I fully understand the stresses of working mothers and caregivers and I'm very aware that I'm not alone in facing these challenges. I'm grateful that I like the work I do and that I have a support system in my husband and friends. Many are not so fortunate, and they struggle to find ways to meet all their responsibilities while spending their "free" time caring for family members.

What advice do you have for someone contemplating a career in gerontology? In a professional position similar to your current position?

I cannot offer advice on the gerontology question, since that is not my direct career path. I can say that working with elders and families in the capacity in which I work them presents interesting challenges. It is tremendously satisfying and rewarding to be a part of such important conversations as people work through some of the biggest challenges and conflicts they face as a family. The important thing about families in conflict is that they have a history and a future—and, usually, a desire to keep their future intact, so they have an incentive to try to work things out, no matter how impossible their issues and conflict feel to them. To see estranged family members hug one another after a mediation is well worth the time and energy that it takes to get to that point. In thinking about whether this would be a good career option for someone, I would recommend first taking a basic mediation training to see if this is a process that is even of interest. To be a good facilitative mediator, one must be able resist the temptation to advise, decide, or tell the mediation participants what the mediator thinks is the best solution. Instead, through questions, discussion, brainstorming, and other appropriate mediation techniques and bringing the appropriate resources and parties to the table, the mediator helps the participants find their own solutions and a path out of the conflict that works best for them. Following the basic training and after having practiced mediating for at least 25 hours, I would recommend taking elder mediation training. One of the most important skills in these cases is learning how to accommodate a person with physical and/or cognitive limitations in the mediation decision-making process, without becoming an advocate for that person; the mediator needs to remain neutral and work with all parties in an impartial manner. Sometimes, the key may be in getting an advocate outside of the family to assure that the mentally or physically frail person is supported or represented at the table. The training is absolutely necessary, in my opinion, to develop these skills–not as a gerontologist or social worker or counselor or lawyer, but as a mediator. There is a big difference in using the skills needed for each occupation, and knowing when and how to wear the different "hats" is a critical factor to success in this field.

Medical Librarian

Basic Description: Medical librarians assist medical and allied health professionals and students, patients, and consumers in their search for information that is relevant to their professional practice, programs of study, and personal health concerns. In doing so, they locate and disseminate medical information and provide instruction on the use of medical-related software programs, databases, online resources, search engines, and search processes that allow library users to locate medical, health care industry, and consumer information that is valid, current, and evidence-based. Medical librarians are increasingly recognized as part of the health care team. In most settings they are generalists. The increased visibility of gerontology and geriatrics as the basis for medical specialties (e.g., geriatric medicine, gerontological nursing, geropsychology, geropsychiatry, geriatric optometry, ophthalmology), allied health fields (e.g., occupational and physical therapy, health care administration, geriatric pharmacy, medical social work), and specialty certifications, however, should increase the potential for more positions in medical librarianship that are specific to these fields.

Education and Experience Requirements: This position requires a master's degree in library and information studies (MLIS), library science (MLS), librarianship (ML), or an MA or MS in library/information studies from an American Library Association (ALA)-accredited program. Health science courses are strongly recommended, and coursework or a degree component in gerontology with a geriatrics orientation is encouraged.

Certification, Licensure, and Continuing Education Requirements: Medical librarians are eligible for membership in the Academy of Health Information Professionals, which is the professional development and career recognition program of the Medical Library Association (MLA). The five levels of Academy membership (provisional, member, senior, distinguished, emeritus) are based on achievements in academic preparation, professional experience, and professional accomplishment.

Core Competencies and Skills Needed:
- Medical terminology
- Health sciences library courses
- Service orientation; passionate about helping others find the information and resources they need

- Knowledge of a broad variety of relevant scholarly and public information sources
- Computer-oriented
- Knowledge of medical, gerontology/geriatric, and health care databases
- Strong interpersonal and collaborative skills
- Excellent communication skills
- Innovative and creative
- Likes to facilitate learning
- Interest in working in medical environment

Compensation: This varies by one's education, experience, the type and location of the workplace, and the level of responsibility.

Workplace(s): These include hospitals, ambulatory care centers, medical and mental health clinics, academic medical centers; college, university, and professional school libraries; university gerontology centers and institutes; consumer health centers; research centers and institutes; medical/health-related industries (e.g., biotechnology, pharmaceutical, insurance); publishing; and federal, state, and local government agencies.

Employment Outlook: Good—due to anticipated high retirement rate among current medical librarians and an increasing focus on gerontology/geriatrics as the population ages. Flexibility about the geographical location for a job will increase one's chances for obtaining a position.

Related Professional Organizations and Web Sites:
- American Library Association (ALA): www.ala.org
- Medical Library Association (MLA): www.mlanet.org
- Academy of Health Information Professionals: www.mlanet.org/academy

---

Music Therapist/Music Therapist-Board Certified (MT-BC)

Basic Description: Music therapists are musicians who are specially trained to use music as a therapeutic tool in addressing the physical, psychological (emotional and cognitive), and social needs of their clients. After assessing the specific strengths, abilities, and needs of a client, the music therapist devises a treatment plan that might include creating and/or performing vocal or instrumental music, moving to music, and/or listening to music. Outcomes of music therapy for clients include facilitation of movement and overall physical rehabilitation; motivation to enter and endure treatment/rehabilitation that is physically or mentally difficult; provision of a calming and emotional supportive environment for clients, their families, and caregivers; and provision of a means of communication and expression of feelings for clients who have difficulty with direct verbal expression. Although music therapists work most frequently as members of interdisciplinary healthcare teams, they also work as individual practitioners in a variety of settings.

Education and Experience Requirements: Music therapists must have a bachelor's or master's degree in music therapy from an American Music Therapy Association (AMTA)-approved academic training program and internship. Gerontology coursework or a degree component is strongly recommended for those who intend to practice primarily with older adults.

Certification, Licensure, and Continuing Education Requirements: Graduates of AMTA-approved degree programs at the bachelor's or master's degree level are eligible to take the certification examination administered by the Certification Board for Music Therapists (CBMT) in order to earn Music Therapist-Board Certified (MT-BC) credentials.

Core Competencies and Skills Needed:
- Genuine interest in people
- Desire to facilitate the empowerment of others
- Ability to establish a caring and professional relationship with clients from diverse backgrounds
- Empathy
- Patience
- Creative, imaginative, and open to new ideas
- Understanding of oneself
- Background in and love of music

Compensation: This varies by one's education, experience, CB-MT credentials, type of professional practice, and the nature of the employment setting. Some positions may be part-time paid by wage or on a fee-for-service basis.

Workplace(s): These include general and psychiatric hospitals, community mental health agencies, rehabilitation centers, day care facilities and adult day programs, skilled and intermediate care facilities, adult foster care homes, dementia care and memory loss units and organizations, hospice, oncology treatment centers, pain/stress management clinics, senior centers, retirement communities, in-home care agencies, other agencies and organizations that serve older adults, correctional settings, private practices, and consulting contractual services.

Employment Outlook: Good—with potential for improvement due to the expansion of the older adult population, the increase in elders' comfort level with therapeutic treatment/intervention, and the addition of and variation in the type of venues in which music therapy can be practiced with older adults.

Related Professional Organizations and Web Sites:
- American Music Therapy Association (AMTA): www.musictherapy.org
- National Coalition of Creative Arts Therapies Associations (NCCATA): www.nccata.org

Nonprofit Community Leadership Training Program Coordinator

Basic Description: Nonprofit organizations are playing a key role in multiple efforts to rebuild a sense of community and neighborhoods in larger cities across the country. The more successful of these organizations have emerged from within the community (compared to programs brought to the community by external organizations). Often the impetus for such a movement comes from chambers of commerce, community action groups, existing networks of service organizations, and/or locally-based foundations with an interest in growing and improving the quality of life and opportunities for citizen involvement in the larger community. For example, one of the premier community leadership training programs in the U.S. began when the local chamber of commerce received funding from a local foundation to create a leadership training program that would last a full year. This successful model led to the development of a nonprofit organization that continues to use the yearlong training model, but with an array of training programs designed to target specific age groups within the community. An organization program coordinator is responsible for a "Third Age Initiative" program for retired and semi-retired community residents who want to be involved in a community development in more in-depth and meaningful ways. They receive leadership training during the year to prepare them to become change agents, policy makers, program developers, and project managers in their neighborhoods and in the larger community. The program coordinator assists with recruitment and training of the older adult volunteers, presents one or more training components, coordinates training workshops and retreats, reviews participant progress, oversees the process and implementation of the various team projects selected by participants, and maintains program records. This responsibility accounts for about 40% of the program coordinator's time, with the remaining 60% allotted to other tasks (e.g., coordination of logistics for some or all organization programs, duties related to basic organizational office maintenance, and organizational liaison with other training or networking programs).

Education and Experience Requirements: Program coordinators require a minimum of a bachelor's degree in community leadership, volunteer administration, or a closely related field. Gerontology coursework or a degree component is strongly recommended for those who wish to administer or coordinate leadership training programs for older adults.

Certification, Licensure, and Continuing Education Requirements: None are required, but relevant certifications and continuing education is encouraged in order to maintain and enhance professional performance.

Core Competencies and Skills Needed:
- Good working knowledge of leadership training models and skills
- Good working knowledge of the community and its resources
- Computer literate in both basic and advanced work-related software programs
- Good interpersonal skills
- Good communication skills (written, oral, listening)
- Good organizational skills
- Ability to prioritize
- Ability to be flexible and adapt easily
- Attentive to details
- Self-directed

Compensation: This varies by one's education, experience, the nature of the employment setting, the geographical location, and is dependent on continued funding for the organization. The position may be part-time and wage-based or combined with responsibilities for two or more of the organization's programs, or for some operational aspects of the organization.

Workplace(s): These include nonprofit organizations, community foundations, community leadership programs, and community outreach programs of foundations and corporations.

Employment Outlook: Limited—but with the potential for improvement as more communities take up similar community-building initiatives.

Related Professional Organizations and Web Sites:
- Leadership Greater Hartford (LGH): www.leadershipgh.org

An Interview with
Julie M. Daly,
Program Director, City Nonprofit
Leadership Training Organization

What is your educational background in gerontology and other disciplines or professional fields? What formal credentials (e.g., completed degrees, certification) do you hold in these fields?

I have a Bachelor of Science (BS) degree in Human Development and Family Studies (2005). I concentrated on adulthood and aging—all of my elective courses dealt with aging in some way.

Briefly describe your gerontology-related career path.

I was influenced at a very early age by my mother, who was a geriatric nurse while I was growing up. I was a foster-grandchild, if you will, to many of her patients, and I became comfortable with older adults through the time I spent at the nursing home where my mother was employed. Later, when I was studying gerontology at the university I attended, my advisor encouraged me to apply for an Association for Gerontology in Higher Education (AGHE) internship. I was selected and completed the internship in Washington, DC during the fall semester of my senior year.

How did you first become interested in your current professional position?

For a long time, I saw myself going into recreational therapy. I was lucky to find the career I did when I graduated with my bachelor's degree because I wasn't ready to go back to school to get certified in recreational therapy. When I returned from Washington, DC to campus for my final semester, an interesting speaker came into one of my adulthood and aging courses. She was the senior program director for a community leadership training organization's Third Age Initiative. She explained the program and the need for meaningful volunteer opportunities for older adults. I knew I wanted to work with older adults in a nonmedical field, so I immediately asked her if they were hiring for her program; I was interviewed the following week. I graduated in May and started work on June 1, so I've been here two years.

What are the most rewarding aspects of your career?

The program we offer begins with five workshops dealing with leadership theory and personality work, as well as showcasing organizations and business in the city. Our participants range in age from 48 to 88 and have come from more than 30 towns throughout the state. After the workshops, the participants break into teams and create a project to tackle an issue that they feel passionate about. They are given a chance to do volunteer work that utilizes their skills and expertise, rather than merely their outstanding envelope-stuffing abilities. All our participants achieve a feeling of self-worth that they've been searching for, and to be able to provide that kind of opportunity is so unbelievably rewarding. I also get to work one-on-one with our participants in many ways and I cherish the personal relationships we develop.

What are the most challenging aspects of your career?

The biggest challenge in my career is juggling a hectic schedule. We are a staff of nine who manage 10 or more programs and there never seems to be enough time in the day to get everything done! Also, recruitment of program participants can require quite a bit of legwork at times, but we always end up with a full class.

Describe a typical workday in your current professional position.

I have two kinds of work day: (1) the days that I am at my desk arranging workshop logistics and assisting with basic office function duties and (2) the days that I am actually attending workshops and tours, troubleshooting, and, sometimes, actually doing some of the training—we use a personality profiler that I have been certified to teach.

How do you balance career and other aspects of your life?

I am very lucky to work in a professional setting with adequate flexibility to allow me to maintain a healthy work-life balance. I have no problem working longer hours during busier weeks because I am able to take time off when

I need it and when the schedule isn't so packed. I've also been able to include my family and friends in some of the events LGH organizes, so I can spend time and share my work life with them at the same time.

What advice do you have for someone contemplating a career in gerontology? In a professional position similar to your current position?

Gerontology is a huge up and coming field. I know scientific discoveries are being made every day, but I find myself more interested in the social aspects that are being recognized more and more as the population is aging. It is my feeling that if you have a passion for working with older adults, you'll be able to find a way to do so that can also incorporate any other skills or talents you may have if you actively look for it. I never expected to be in the career I am in, but now that I am, I can't see myself anywhere else. I think the best advice is to keep your eyes and ears open; read the newspaper, attend local lectures, find out about what is going on in the field of gerontology. You are bound to find a position that fits your interests and skills.

Nurse Case Manager

Basic Description: Nurse Case Managers work in full- or part-time positions as members of multidisciplinary teams to provide case management services to older adults living in the community or healthcare-related facilities. They conduct comprehensive nursing assessments and oversee cost-effective service plans; visit clients in their own homes; conduct regular health monitoring and verification of services; determine the quality and effectiveness of services being provided to clients; prepare written, technical, and statistical reports and correspondence; maintain electronic and physical clinical records; conduct outreach; develop informational materials; contact potential referrals; represent the agency in the public and with care providers; provide supervision to interns and students; participate with other members of the clinical team during meetings and trainings; provide intake and referral coverage when needed; and perform other related special projects as assigned.

Education and Experience Requirements: This position requires either a Master's of Science in Nursing (MSN) degree, plus one year of casework experience in a community with a considerable 60+ population, or a Bachelor's of Science in Nursing (BSN) degree, plus 3 years of similar casework experience.

Certification, Licensure, and Continuing Education Requirements: Nurse case managers must have a registered nurse (RN) degree from an accredited school of nursing, with a certificate in public health nursing (PHN). They must meet licensure requirements, including having a valid driver's license, in the state where their professional practice occurs, and they must meet the continuing education requirements mandated by the state licensing board and/ or their employing agency.

Core Competencies and Skills Needed:
- Good working knowledge of the principles and practices of case management services, including: interviewing, diagnostic assessment, service plan development, service coordination, and care monitoring
- Excellent English communication skills; capacity to communicate verbally in other languages may be preferred or required
- Ability to work in a multidisciplinary/interdisciplinary team

- Familiarity with word processing, spreadsheet, and electronic charting programs

Compensation: This varies by one's education, experience, the nature of the employing agency, and the geographical location. Some positions may be part-time positions with wage earnings and prorated benefits.

Workplace(s): These include aging services divisions of a county or city human services departments, Area Agencies on Aging, visiting nurse or home care organizations/agencies, and in-home hospice programs.

Employment Outlook: Excellent—as demand for nurses, including nurse case managers, exceeds supply.

Related Professional Organizations and Web Sites:
- American Nurses Association (ANA): www.ana.org
- Visiting Nurses Association (VNA): www.vna.org

Nutrition Educator

Basic Description: Nutrition educators offer information about good nutrition, dietary needs, food sanitation and safety, food purchasing and meal preparation, and other food-related behaviors and issues to older adults, their families and caregivers, and to professionals who provide direct services to older adults through a wide variety of venues. Nutrition educators with gerontological interests who belong to the Society of Nutrition Educators (SNE) may participate in the organization's Healthy Aging Division, which is a network designed to stimulate research on and provide professional services to maximize a nutrition-based quality of life for older adults through nutrition education, proper dietary behavior, and development of public and private policies to support healthy aging through nutrition. Some nutrition educators also are registered dietitians (RDs) who belong to the American Dietetic Association (ADA) and participate in one or more of the ADA's Dietetic Practice Groups (DPGs) related to nutrition education (e.g., Dietetic Educators and Practitioners, Food and Culinary Professionals, Gerontological Nutritionists, and Nutrition Education for the Public).

Education and Experience Requirements: Becoming a nutrition educator requires a bachelor's degree in nutrition or dietetics from an accredited institution of higher education. Gerontology coursework or a degree component is strongly recommended for those who intend to work predominantly with elders. A PhD in nutrition or dietetics is required for those who wish to teach in higher education or work in research centers/institutes.

Certification, Licensure, and Continuing Education Requirements: Nutrition educators must comply with requirements of their employing agencies. Continuing education is strongly recommended to stay updated on relevant information and new research findings nutrition and aging.

Core Competencies and Skills Needed:
- Working knowledge of adult learning theory and adult education teaching methodologies
- Good oral and written communication skills; good listener
- Ability to translate scientific knowledge to learners from diverse educational, socioeconomic, and cultural backgrounds
- Commitment to learner-centered educational practice

Compensation: This varies by one's education, experience, the nature of the employment setting, and the geographic location. Some positions may be part-time and wage-based, or paid on fee-for-service basis.

Workplace(s): These include school-based adult and community education programs; older adult educational programs and settings, such as senior centers and institutes for learning in retirement; organizations specific to physical and/or mental health conditions, such as the American Diabetes Association (ADA) education centers and Alzheimer's Association; public health departments; wellness and fitness centers; weight management programs, centers, and organizations; academia; research centers and institutes; medical clinics and health-care centers; newspapers, magazines and other publications; and cooperative extension service programs and publications.

Employment Outlook: Promising—due to increased public interest in nutrition, more emphasis on diet and nutrition as prevention and treatment tools in health care, the increase in the older adult population, and elders who are living longer and healthier. The actual demand for nutrition educators working with gerontological clientele has not yet been established.

Related Professional Organizations and Web Sites:
- American Dietetic Association (ADA): www.eatright.org
- Society for Nutrition Education (SNE): www.sne.org
- Informal Interest Group on Nutrition, Gerontological Society of America (GSA): www.geron.org

Occupational Therapist (OT) Occupational Therapy Assistant (OTA)

Basic Description: Occupational Therapists (OTs) and Occupational Therapy Assistants (OTAs) assist their clients and patients with physical, cognitive, or emotional limitations in ways that allow them to stay active in occupations, accomplish activities of daily living (ADLs) and instrumental activities of daily living (IADLs), participate socially, engage in productive activity (such as employment or volunteering), and be involved in other activities that provide quality of life (such as hobbies and avocations) for older adults. Licensed **OTs** work independently with clients/patients or as members of multidisciplinary health care or social services teams. **OTAs** work under the direction and supervision of licensed OTs. They are trained to assess the client/patient's ability to accomplish a desired task or activity, then offer recommendations for changes in the related physical environment(s) and assist clients/patients in adapting or learning new behaviors and routines. They work with issues of sensory loss (such as hearing loss and visual impairment), dysphagia (eating or swallowing disorders), fall prevention, mobility limitations, and role transitions (such as retirement and widowhood). In 2004 the AOTA president identified six emerging "hot practice areas" for occupational therapy professionals. Five of these areas are directly related to OT and OTA work with older adults: support for "aging in place" (including the design of new homes or the modification of existing ones), older driver rehabilitation, community health and wellness initiatives, ergonomics consulting with older workers and their employers, and technology/assistive-device development and consulting.

Education and Experience Requirements: OTs require a Bachelor's or Master's degree in Occupational Therapy that includes a supervised clinical internship. A master's degree is preferred and is required for clinical practice. A doctoral degree is required for teaching in higher education. OTAs require an associate's degree or bachelor's degree in occupational therapy that includes a supervised clinical internship. Gerontology coursework or a degree component is encouraged for OTs and OTAs whose practice is primarily with older adults.

Certification, Licensure, and Continuing Education Requirements: OTs and OTAs must pass a national examination to be eligible for licensure and meet state requirements for licensure in the state where professional practice occurs. Voluntary board certification of competencies and indicators in gerontology, mental health, and physical rehabilitation are available for OTs who meet the requirements. Voluntary specialty certification of competencies and indicators in driving and community mobility, environmental modification, low vision, and feeding, eating, and swallowing are available for OTs and OTAs who meet the requirements.

Core Competencies and Skills Needed:
- Ability to instill confidence in clients and patients
- Ability to direct or instruct clients and patients with clarity, gentleness, and firmness
- Patience
- Strong interpersonal skills
- Excellent verbal and written communication skills; attentive listener
- Attentive to detail in therapeutic practice
- Ability to maintain accurate patient and client records
- Ability to respond and adapt quickly to client and patient needs during therapy sessions
- OTs: Ability to competently support the development of and supervise OTAs and interns
- OTAs: Open to guidance and instruction from supervising OTs; ability to follow directions as instructed

Compensation: This varies by one's education, experience, certifications, the nature of the employment setting, level of responsibility, and geographical location.

Workplace(s): For OTs and OTAs, these include hospitals, rehabilitation centers, outpatient clinics, long-term care and assisted living facilities, senior centers and other community-based settings that serve older adults, patients' homes, and home care agencies. For OTs only, workplaces can also include private practices and consulting that is frequently related to one of the "hot practice areas" noted above.

Employment Outlook: Excellent—especially for OTs in private practice and consulting, due to strong support for "aging in place" and independent living goals for older adults.

Related Professional Organizations and Web Sites:
- American Occupational Therapy Association (AOTA): www.aota.org

Older Adult System of Care Director

Basic Description: Comprehensive systems of care are networks of services and programs offered by multiple organizations and agencies through a single coordinating organization or agency. This is an emerging model for the provision of services to elders that allows older adults to access services at a "one stop services center." So far, these networks tend to focus on one aspect of care, usually mental health and substance abuse services, gerontological/ geriatric services, or physical health care services (although there appears to be at least some overlap in the existing networks). If the network services persons of many ages, the Older Adult System of Care Director position is likely to be a second tier administrative post with a direct line of report to the top network administrator. If only older adults are served, this position may be the top administrative post. Regardless, the older adult system of care director: plans, organizes, and directs services provided to older adults; provides leadership in the development and administration of organizational policy, system design, and program development; develops and implements "best practices" in the provision and delivery of services; develops and implements culturally competent programs and strategies in effective outreach, engagement, wellness and recovery; assures interagency and intraagency collaboration and integration of services; negotiates and manages contracts, program services agreements, and interagency agreements; participates in the formation of recommendations for the allocation of available funds for both county and community-operated and contracted services; represents the agency at local, state, and national events and conferences; represents and provides liaison services for the agency or organization at relevant state and federal governmental units, agencies, and departments; and represents departmental positions, strategies, and needs to the agency or organization's policy and/or advisory board(s) and to relevant community/county boards and departments.

Education and Experience Requirements: Educationally, these positions require a master's degree in public health administration, business administration, clinical psychology, social work, nursing, or a closely related field. Gerontology coursework or a degree component is strongly recommended. Regarding experience, these positions require 5 or more years of full-time administrative/

management postgraduate experience in community organization, planning, and evaluation; budget, fiscal, and personnel management in a community health, mental health, or medical setting that provides services to older adults and their families; and one or more full-time years of experience in a geriatric setting (an associate's degree or higher in gerontology may substitute for 1 or more years of experience).

Certification, Licensure, and Continuing Education Requirements: A valid license or clinical licensure is required by the state in which the practice occurs for some professional backgrounds (e.g., social work, clinical psychology, or nursing).

Core Competencies and Skills Needed:
- Good working knowledge of administrative principles, practices, and techniques of county, state, and federal physical and/or mental health systems relative to providing services to older adults
- Understand principles and practices of governmental budgeting, funding, and grant/contract management; ability to develop, analyze, and monitor budgets
- Recognize methods of effective community organization and its role in physical and/or mental health treatment and prevention programs
- Familiar with principles and best practices in the delivery of culturally competent physical and/or mental health services to older adults
- Familiar with principles and best practices of wellness and recovery
- Good working knowledge of program evaluation methodologies and management analysis
- Good working knowledge of clinical standards of practice and licensure requirements
- Effective written and oral communication skills; good listening skills
- Effective leadership and sound decision making skills
- Good planning, prioritization, and organizational skills
- Ability to establish and maintain cooperative work relationships with in-agency departments, other agencies, and the community

Compensation: This varies by one's educational background, experience, the nature of the agency, the level of the position in the network's administrative hierarchy, and the geographical location.

Workplace(s): These include city or county governmental units; community- or county-based human services, medical care, and behavioral health agencies or organizations.

Employment Outlook: Promising—but demand is not yet determined for this emerging career position. Employment opportunities should improve as more "one stop service centers" are created to meet the needs of the rapidly growing elderly population.

Related Professional Organizations and Web Sites: None yet identified.

Ombudsperson

Basic Description: Ombudspersons actively protect the rights of vulnerable individuals and intercede on their behalf in situations in which injustice is potential, suspected, or real. They work with elders in cases related to physical and/or mental frailty, socioeconomic disadvantage, elder abuse and neglect, consumer fraud, caregiving, placement in long-term care facilities, medical care, family disputes, and other situations that increase the vulnerability of elders. Access to the services of an ombudsperson are written into the laws and regulations for some facilities (e.g., hospitals, long-term care facilities) and are provided without extra charge for clients of those facilities. In some cases the courts order and designate an ombudsperson for the vulnerable elder. Although "ombudsman" and "ombudsperson" are common titles for persons who serve this function, an increasing number of organizations and facilities are using the position title of "advocate" or "elder advocate"; sometimes the title refers to the professional background of the person fulfilling this role, such as "legal advocate" or "nurse advocate." Regardless of the title, ombudspersons mediate disputes, investigate alleged or suspected injustices, and work to assure that the resolution of problems is fair to the vulnerable elder.

Education and Experience Requirements: This position requires a bachelor's degree or higher in social work, psychology/clinical psychology, law, or a closely related field. Gerontology coursework or a degree component is strongly recommended, and mediation training is encouraged.

Certification, Licensure, and Continuing Education Requirements: Ombudspersons must meet the requirements of the state in which their practice occurs and of the employing agency.

Core Competencies and Skills Needed:
- Knowledge of the dynamics of interpersonal situations in which neglect, abuse, fraud, and other injustices against vulnerable elders can occur
- Working knowledge of the rules, regulations, and laws related to injustices against vulnerable elders
- Casework skills
- Mediation skills
- Good listening skills

- Good oral and written communication skills
- Good interpersonal skills

Compensation: This varies by one's education, experience, the nature of the work setting, and the geographical location.

Workplace(s): These include hospitals/medical centers, medical and mental health clinics/practices, long-term care and assisted living facilities, "senior living" communities and residences, police departments, law firms, courts, consumer organizations, and domestic violence shelters.

Employment Outlook: Good—with an anticipated increase in demand due to the rapid growth of the elderly population and the enactment of additional protective legislation specific to older adults.

Related Professional Organizations and Web Sites:
- AARP National Legal Training Project (NLTP): http://aarpnltp.grovesite.com

---

Physical Therapist (PT) Physical Therapist Assistant (PTA)

Basic Description: Physical Therapists (PTs) diagnose and treat older adult clients with medical problems or health-care issues that prevent or restrict their ability to move about normally and perform other common functions of daily life. Treatment goals include the promotion of mobility, reduction of pain, restoration of function, and prevention of disability. Through fitness and wellness programs, PTs work to prevent loss of mobility before it occurs. PTs are licensed to provide the full range of physical therapy services as they work in conjunction with physicians and surgeons or as members of interdisciplinary medical/health care teams. They may also practice independently in nonmedical settings, such as fitness and wellness centers. **Physical Therapist Assistants (PTAs)**, under the direction and supervision of licensed PTs, may provide physical therapy services to older adult clients/patients. Their services, for example, might include teaching or assisting with therapy exercises to enhance mobility, strength, and coordination; training clients/patients to use mobility aids (such as crutches, canes, or walkers); doing therapeutic massages; and using physical agents and electrotherapy (such as electrical stimulation or ultrasound) as part of the treatment plan developed by the supervising PT.

Education and Experience Requirements: PTs require a Master's (MPT) or Doctor's (DPT) degree in Physical Therapy; **PTAs** require an Associate's degree (APT) in Physical Therapy

Certification, Licensure, and Continuing Education Requirements: PTs must pass a state-administered national examination and meet any other requirements of the state in which the professional practice occurs. PTs who are currently licensed to practice in a state or jurisdiction of the U.S. and have completed at least 2,000 hours (with at least 25% of the hours completed in the past 3 years) of clinical practice in the geriatrics specialty area qualify to sit for the Specialist Certification Examination in Geriatrics. Recertification is required every 10 years. PTAs must meet licensure and certification or registration requirements in the state in which the professional practice occurs.

Core Competencies and Skills Needed:
- Personal physical fitness and full range of mobility
- Good interpersonal skills
- Good verbal communication and listening skills
- Patience
- Ability to offer instruction and direction clearly
- Ability to model therapeutic techniques
- Ability to be gentle, but firm in interaction with clients/patients

Compensation: This varies by one's education, experience, the practice setting, the nature and level of the position, and the geographical location.

Workplace(s): These include outpatient clinics or offices, in-patient rehabilitation facilities, hospitals, long-term care and assisted living facilities, home health care agencies, patients' homes, education or research centers, hospices, occupational environments, fitness centers, sports training facilities, and retirement communities.

Employment Outlook: Good—and appears to be improving for both PTs and PTAs. Anticipated improvement through the next few decades will be due to an increase in the elderly population and more elders being involved in physical fitness and sports activities.

Related Professional Organizations and Web Sites:
- American Physical Therapy Association (APTA): www.apta.org
- Commission on Accreditation in Physical Therapy Education (CAPTE): www.apta.org

Recreational Therapist Certified Therapeutic Recreation Specialist (CTRS)

Basic Description: Through recreation services, education, and treatment, **Recreational Therapists** and **Certified Therapeutic Recreation Specialists** (CTRSs) help ill, frail, and disabled older adults develop and use leisure activities to maintain or improve their physical and/or mental health, level of function, independence and quality of life. Recreational therapists assess the physical, mental, emotional, and social function level of their clients to determine client needs, interests, and abilities. Such assessment is the basis for the design and implementation of individualized and/or group treatment, education, and program plans used to help clients and patients become active and informed partners in their health care; cope better with the stress of the condition(s) they are experiencing; achieve and maintain optimal levels of independence, well-being, and productivity; and reenter the mainstream of their individual, family, and community life. Therapeutic recreation specialists also provide recreational opportunities and leisure activities that can reduce the need for medical care services, minimize health care costs, slow or prevent decline in one or more aspects of the overall health status, and improve the quality of life for their clients and patients. They often serve as part of an interdisciplinary care team. Some therapeutic recreations specialists advance into supervisory and administrative positions, become consultants for health or social service agencies, or move into teaching and research positions in higher education.

Education and Experience Requirements: These positions require the minimum of a bachelor's degree from an accredited recreational therapy program, including a supervised internship. Graduate-level coursework or a master's degree may be required in some settings. Gerontology coursework or a degree component is strongly recommended for professionals who work with older adults. Supervisory, administrative, college teaching, and research positions require the completion of a master's or doctoral degree.

Certification, Licensure, and Continuing Education Requirements: Recreational therapists must hold a current Certified Therapeutic Recreation Specialist (CTRS) credential issued by the National Council for Therapeutic Recreation Certification (NCTRC), an independent credentialing body. Becoming credentialed requires a bachelor's degree from an accredited program and a passing score on the national certification examination. Recertification is required every 5 years and can be achieved by repassing the national certification examination or through a combination of professional work experience in therapeutic recreation and continuing education related to the NCTRC job analysis. Recreational therapists must comply with any legal requirements for licensure, registration, or certification appropriate to their practice settings, although only Utah currently requires licensure for recreational therapists.

Core Competencies and Skills Needed:
- Comfortable working with ill or disabled persons
- Patience, tact, and persuasiveness
- Commitment to a holistic approach to client and patient care
- Ability to use ingenuity, imagination, and creativity in adapting activities to fit the individual needs of clients and patients
- Sense of humor
- Enjoys an array of recreational and leisure activities
- Good organizational skills
- Good oral and written communication skills
- Ability to work cooperatively and collaboratively
- Good physical coordination

Compensation: This varies by one's education, experience, the nature of the practice setting, and the geographical location.

Workplace(s): These include acute care hospitals and medical centers, rehabilitation centers, long-term and nursing care facilities, community recreation centers, group homes, senior centers, community mental health centers, correctional facilities, and private practices.

Employment Outlook: Excellent—faster than average growth is expected due to the anticipated expansion of the need for long-term care and physical/psychiatric rehabilitation for older adults.

Related Professional Organizations and Web Sites:
- National Recreation and Park Association (NRPA): www.nrpa.org
- National Therapeutic Recreation Society (NTRS, a unit of NRPA): www.nrpa.org
- National Council for Therapeutic Recreation Certification (NCTRC): www.nctrc.org
- **Proposed Interest Group on Recreational Therapists, Gerontological Society of America (GSA): www.geron.org**

An Interview with Maureen Lee Pawlak, Certified Therapeutic Recreation Specialist, Nursing Home

What is your educational background in gerontology and other disciplines or professional fields? What formal credentials (e.g., completed degrees, certification) do you hold in these fields?

I received my Bachelor of Science (BS) degree in Therapeutic Recreation, with an undergraduate minor in gerontology, in 2001. I earned my Certified Therapeutic Recreation Specialist (CTRS) credentials through the National Council of Therapeutic Recreation Certification (NCTRC).

Briefly describe your gerontology-related career path.

Many of my college courses in therapeutic recreation and gerontology required fieldwork. For one of my gerontology courses, I had to team up with another student to provide respite for a local caregiver. His wife had Alzheimer's disease, and we were to provide "meaningful activities" for her while her husband took a break. This was a wonderful experience! Most of my fieldwork, however, was related to therapeutic recreation and I met these requirements in a variety of settings, including a hospital physical rehabilitation center, various assisted living centers, a memory care residence on the campus of the hospital, and at a long-term care center. In the fall of 2001, I completed my 15 week required practicum for therapeutic recreation at a Veteran's Administration (VA) Hospital Extended Care Center. In 2002, I started off my career as recreational therapy assistant at a nursing home and then moved up to recreational therapy director at this same facility about two years later. Recently, I was hired as the recreational therapy director at a privately-owned, assisted and independent living facility, with an onsite memory care unit, and a bed capacity that is slightly larger than the nursing home. Until I move into this new position, I'm still working at the nursing home and will continue to do so on a contingency basis after I start my new job.

How did you first become interested in your current professional position?

I first realized that I wanted to pursue therapeutic recreation while flipping through the booklet of possible majors and minors at my university. I was undeclared for the first three years of college. For years, I wanted to do something related to recreation, but I wasn't sure what area. What initially interested me was the outdoors, due to the wonderful camping experiences I was into at that time. I am also very altruistic by nature, and I thought this was a good fit.

What are the most rewarding aspects of your career?

The most rewarding aspect of my career is feeling that every day I am truly making a positive difference in someone's life—even if I am having "one of those days." My job is to maximize the quality of residents' lives. When I think about it, this is an amazing job to have. Also, with the experiences I've had, watching myself grow professionally has been surprisingly rewarding—this has just surfaced more recently.

What are the most challenging aspects of your career?

Sometimes, I feel I'm being pulled in a million directions at once! Working in a nursing home can be very intense, and burn out is not uncommon. It can be very stressful, sometimes sad. I've gotten very attached to a few residents and, when they passed away, it was a powerful experience for me. Also, most people don't understand what recreational therapy is. Recreational therapy is used to maximize a resident's potential and/or rehabilitate a client through recreational activities. This will look different in different settings, which might be confusing to some. So, I must always explain my field and advocate for it.

Describe a typical workday in your current professional position.

A typical day as a CTRS in a nursing home varies quite a bit. My day consists of: a morning meeting (with the administrator and other department heads; we get reports on residents and communicate with each other about various things); completing the Minimum Data Set (MDS), an interdisciplinary tool used to assess each resident, and documentation on residents; doing some activity programming and making phone calls. Some days I'm "on the floor," which means I'm leading activity groups, working one-on-one therapeutic activities with residents, and doing sensory stimulation. On certain days, there are Care Conferences, which are meetings with the resident, interdisciplinary team (nursing, social services, dietary, and therapeutic recreation), and family member(s). Other meetings pop up as well, such as Patients at Risk (PAR) and Quality Assurance (QA). I tend to shop weekly for supplies (bingo prizes, arts/crafts, food, and anything else we might need for groups). I do the calendar of events and scheduling monthly. I am also in charge of training and supervising volunteers and the recreational therapy staff. Weather permitting, I take residents on outings. There are many other tasks or responsibilities that fall into my workday, such as being a resident advocate, assisting a resident with putting their shoes on, or answering alarm doors. My typical workday varies quite a bit—this is kind of nice, actually. Some days, though, can be very hectic.

How do you balance career and other aspects of your life?

I'm working on balancing my career and other aspects of my life. There used to be much more carryover from work to my personal life, but I've learned to let some of those stresses go. I often think of ideas for programs and interventions or sometimes do work-related shopping on my own time, so there is some crossover. I definitely take my work home at times. I feel, though, like my career is what makes me the most proud at this time, so I am emotionally and mentally tied to what I do for a living—and that feels okay for now.

What advice do you have for someone contemplating a career in gerontology? In a professional position similar to your current position?

My advice to someone contemplating a field in gerontology is to get experience in a variety of settings—through volunteerism, jobs, wherever you can—to see if it's for you Also, I think one of the biggest mistakes people make is to stereotype older adults as "wise," "grumpy," or "lonely." There are so many variations in people—in personality, intelligence, kindness, and abilities. I sometimes feel like this should be so obvious, but then I remember the people I've been hanging out with for so many years. Be prepared to break down some barriers. As far as recreational therapy, again, it is very important to try out different settings, especially in school and early in your career, to get a feel for where your niche is. There are many options. Also, since many people don't understand what recreational therapy is, advocate for yourself and for this professional field.

Registered Dietitian (RD) Dietitian Technician, Registered (DTR)

Basic Description: Registered Dietitians (RDs) are food and nutrition experts who assess patient and client dietary needs, develop dietary plans appropriate to the patient/client's health needs, and monitor dietary treatment plans. The specific focus of their professional practice depends on their primary Dietetic Practice Group (DPG). For dietitians working in gerontological or geriatric settings, for example, the Gerontological Nutritionists DPG includes practitioners who provide and manage dietary/nutrition services or programs for older adults through community-based agencies and organizations, home care agencies, healthcare and residential facilities, and research centers and institutes. Other relevant DPG affiliations might be with consultant dietitians in health care facilities, dietetics in physical medicine and rehabilitation, medical nutrition practice group, public health/community nutrition, or with DPGs related to specific physical or mental health conditions, such as diabetes care and education, dietetics in developmental and psychiatric disorders, HIV/AIDS, oncology, renal dietitian, weight management, or sports, cardiovascular, and wellness nutritionists. **Dietitian Technicians, Registered (DTRs)** are food and nutrition practitioners who work in conjunction with registered dietitians or under the supervision of other food and nutrition experts in a variety of for-profit, nonprofit, food industry and governmental agencies. Their DPG affiliation is with the Dietetic Technicians in Practice.

Education and Experience Requirements: RDs require a Bachelor's degree in Dietetics from an accredited university/college, including coursework approved by the Commission on Accreditation for Dietetics Education (CADE) of the American Dietetics Association; a CADE-accredited 6–12 month supervised practice experience; and a national examination administered by the Commission on Dietetic Registrations. DTRs require at least a 2 year associate's degree from an accredited community college, college, or university, including coursework approved by the Commission on Accreditation for Dietetics Education of the American Dietetic Association; 450 hours of supervised practice experience; and passing the national examination administered by the Commission on Dietetic Registration.

Certification, Licensure, and Continuing Education Requirements:
Some RDs hold certification(s) awarded through CDR (ADA's credentialing agency) in specialized areas of practice. RDs and DTRs must comply with the state regulatory laws for dietitians, nutrition practitioners, and dietetic technicians in the state where their professional practice occurs. RDs and DTRs must complete continuing professional education to maintain their registration.

Core Competencies and Skills Needed:
- Good oral and written communication skills
- Computer literacy appropriate to maintenance of patient/client records
- Dietary assessment and analysis skills
- Good organizational skills
- Ability to work cooperatively and collaboratively in dietitian-dietetic technician teams and/or interdisciplinary health care teams
- Ability to translate dietary and nutrition information to healthcare colleagues, patients/clients, caregivers, and public

Compensation: This varies by type of registration (RD or DTR), one's education, experience, certification (RD), type of practice, the nature of the employment setting, the scope of responsibility, and the supply of RDs/DTRs available for employment in the immediate geographical location.

Workplace(s): For RDs these include hospitals (in-patient and acute care) HMOs, long-term care facilities, and other healthcare facilities, agencies, and organizations; academia; research centers/institutes; medical clinics and ambulatory care centers; and private practices; and consultancies (to healthcare facilities or individual clients). DTRs may work with dietitians in hospitals, HMOs, clinics, and other healthcare centers, or they may work in community and public health settings, such as daycare centers, correctional facilities, and weight management clinics; in the food and nutrition industry, such as food management, vending, or distribution companies; in food service settings such as retirement communities, home-delivered meals programs, and congregate meal sites for older adults; and in settings related to menu development, food sanitation, and food safety.

Employment Outlook: Good—for both RDs and DTRs, with expected growth at the same rate as is average for all occupations through 2010 due to increased focus on disease prevention, growth of the elderly population, and increased public interest in nutrition. Growth is anticipated for positions in long-term and residential care facilities and physician clinics, but with little or no change in hospital-based opportunities.

Related Professional Organizations and Web Sites:
- American Dietetic Association (ADA): www.eatright.org

Registered Financial Gerontologist (RFG)

Basic Description: Registered Financial Gerontologists (RFGs) are professionals from an array of related fields (e.g., accounting, banking, insurance, financial/retirement planning, development and fundraising, social work) who assist elders and their families with developing and maintaining appropriate financial strategies so as to achieve their changing financial needs and goals across the lifespan.

Education and Experience Requirements: RFGs must complete the American Institute of Financial Gerontology (AIFG) training program, which includes required courses on wealth-span planning, basic processes of aging, serving older clients, and financial longevity, plus elective courses on subjects such as families and aging, aging network and long-term care delivery systems, long-term care solutions, financial preparedness for later life, and/or successful marketing to the 50+ consumer. Becoming a RFG also requires completing the AIFG-approved service learning activity, passing a comprehensive exam, and agreeing to an ethical practice pledge.

Certification, Licensure, and Continuing Education Requirements: Admission to a RFG training program requires the verification of one's existing financial background (in the form of a license, degree, or verifiable professional experience). The annual renewal of an active RFG designation requires additional continuing education coursework, a service learning activity, renewal of the RFG pledge, and payment of a membership fee.

Core Competencies and Skills Needed:
- Financial status assessment skills
- Knowledge of current legal/regulatory mandates related to financial planning
- Commitment to client-centered professional practice
- Good mathematical skills
- Excellent interpersonal communication skills
- Ability to maintain confidentiality about client information
- Comfortable working with two or more generations of the client's family
- Adherence to legal and ethical professional practice

Compensation: This varies by type of professional practice, one's education, experience, the nature of the employment setting, level of position, and the geographical location.

Workplace(s): These include accounting firms, banks, law firms, insurance agencies, private consulting firms, and mortgage agencies.

Employment Outlook: Excellent—due to the rapid growth in the older adult population, stronger interest in planning for financial security, and an emerging focus on wealth management that encompasses all aspects of life.

Related Professional Organizations and Web Sites:
- American Institute of Financial Gerontology (AIFG): www.aifg.org

An Interview with Rosanne Grande, Registered Financial Gerontologist (RFG)

What is your educational background in gerontology and other disciplines or professional fields? What formal credentials (e.g., completed degrees, certification) do you hold in these fields?

I have a Bachelor of Arts degree in Human Relations/Psychology and an Associate's degree in Applied Science. In addition, I completed [a] certificate program in financial planning and a College for Financial Planning Para-Planner program. I am designated as a Certified Financial Planner (CFP) by the CFP Board of Standards. My gerontology background was gained through completing the requirements to become a Registered Financial Gerontologist (RFG) through the American Institute of Financial Gerontology (AIFG) and a Certified Senior Advisor (CSA), conferred by the Society of Certified Senior Advisors. I also hold a New York State Life, Accident, and Health Licensure. Although I currently work for a fee-only firm and do not sell product or earn commissions, I maintain this licensure to keep myself informed on the insurance industry, and, on behalf of our clients, to be aware of relevant insurance products.

Briefly describe your gerontology-related career path.

I have always had an interest in "seniors." My parents had me later in life (45 years, Mom, and 47 years, Dad), so I had older aunts, uncles, siblings, and other relatives. I took care of my mother in my home for ten years, nursing her through various illnesses until she passed away. In dealing with our client base, we noticed that our retired clients were dealing with issues, both financial and physical, with living parents. At one meeting, we were doing a plan update for a client and the topic of life changes was discussed. They told us that they were now financially responsible for the wife's parents who had run out of funds. To move the parents into their home, the client couple needed to do some renovations to make it "senior safe." The clients, however, were only marginally funded. This led me to review our client base and I realized that a major portion of our clients were retired and had responsibility for one or both sets of living parents. I wanted to ensure that we had the "service" in place to help our clients and their parents. This led me to pursue the CSA and RFG designations in addition to my CFP designation.

How did you first become interested in your current professional position?

I had always worked in various capacities of the financial services field, part-time while in college and then full-time after graduation. When I was hired at a financial advising firm in 1991, my boss encouraged me to pursue life and securities licenses. In addition, a good friend did the financial planning at the firm and that helped to spark my interest. I truly enjoy helping others and helping them achieve their goals. This became even more apparent when I came to work at my current place of employment, a financial advising and investments firm. I was the first employee and began taking the CFP classes at C.W. Post University. The owner of the company was very encouraging and provided me with the best opportunity to pursue my goal of becoming a CFP.

What are the most rewarding aspects of your career?

I love helping people and their families. In our practice, we see all kinds of folks who need help—from the college planning for their newborn to helping with aging parents. We had a client who was taking care of her mother at home, but could no longer do so. With some of my contacts, we helped get her mom into a well-run nursing home. This provided my client with the peace of mind that she needed, assured her mom would have a better quality of life, and rewarded me with the satisfaction of knowing that I helped a client.

What are the most challenging aspects of your career?

There are many challenges in working with clients since each client has her or his own situation, and no matter how similar, no two situations are alike. The challenge is trying to help a client articulate their goals, either financial or personal, and be able to help them, her or him in the pursuit of these goals.

Describe a typical workday in your current professional position.

Believe it or not, no day is typical. Everyday is a new adventure. Because I oversee the "client services function" for my company, however, I regularly meet with prospective clients to assess their financial needs and wants, then develop, implement and monitor a written financial plan.

How do you balance career and other aspects of your life?

I just make sure that I give my best when I am at work and give my best to my fiancé and our friends when I am with them. I always leave some time for myself to reflect on all the good that there is in life—to reflect on the positive, not the negative.

What advice do you have for someone contemplating a career in gerontology? In a professional position similar to your current position?

Individuals who wish to work in positions related to financial gerontology need to recognize that their "client" might include both the client with whom they will work directly, and potentially, one or more "indirect clients" from other generations of the direct client's family (e.g., the direct client's parents, children, and/or grandchildren). As a result, it would be helpful to have some educational background related to intergenerational and multigenerational relationships within aging families. Current and future clients of financial gerontologists will be looking to financial advisors for help in all aspects of their lives. This will require a broader and more in-depth understanding of the client's interests and needs related to factors such as housing, health and medical care, employment, caregiving, lifestyle preferences, and overall quality of life.

Researcher
Research Associate
Research Assistant

Basic Description: **Researchers** are the primary investigators for qualitative and quantitative studies that are conducted to add to the base of gerontological knowledge; describe the elderly population; understand change across time for individuals and age cohorts as they move into and through later life; determine patterns of stability and change with age; identify, test, and evaluate interventions and treatments; evaluate programs and services; and learn about other aspects of aging and the elderly population. Researchers are responsible for the overall design of the study, including determination of the theoretical base for the study, hypotheses to be tested and/or research questions to be asked, study subjects and the processes through which they will be involved in the study, and the procedures or strategies to be used for data gathering and analysis. When the study is completed, they will disseminate the findings through written products (e.g., research reports, books or book chapters, professional journal articles) and in-person presentations to study stakeholders and professional conferences. Gerontological researchers come from a wide variety of academic disciplines and professions; most hold doctorates in their fields. **Research Associates** work alongside researchers to assist in the design, implementation, and analysis phases of the research project; serve as project managers; coordinate project team activity; maintain communication with institutional, funding, and national/international project partners; and assist with the preparation of reports and dissemination of information about the study and its results. Research associates also have diverse backgrounds, but most frequently have master's degrees or are doctoral students in the field(s) directly related to the research project on which they are working. **Research Assistants** commonly are students in masters' and doctoral degree programs in the fields relevant to a specific research project; as such, they are often considered to be "researchers-in-training." They primarily assist with the design, conduct data analysis phases of the research project, and may be involved in the reporting and dissemination of data.

Education and Experience Requirements: Researchers require a doctoral degree in gerontology or a closely related discipline or professional field. Completion of a postdoctoral fellowship is encouraged and experience with research of the type being conducted is expected. **Research Associates** require a minimum of a master's degree or higher in gerontology or a closely related discipline or professional field; experience with research of the type being conducted is strongly recommended. **Research Assistants** require the minimum of a bachelor's degree in gerontology or a closely related discipline or professional field, plus the successful completion of research design/methodology and statistics coursework.

Certification, Licensure, and Continuing Education Requirements: Researchers must meet the requirements of the employing center, institute, department or agency, and/or funding agency(ies). Requirements may be more stringent for governmental or private research centers and institutes, especially those that work in medical, biological, and health-related research.

Core Competencies and Skills Needed:
- Demonstrated competence in research design and methodology
- Demonstrated competence in the use of a broad range of statistical processes
- Excellent foundation of knowledge related to topic of research project/study
- Ability to concentrate and stay focused
- Good written and oral communication skills
- Ability to work collaboratively
- Ability to supervise or be supervised

Compensation: This varies by level of position, one's education, experience, the nature of the employment setting, and funding resources for a specific research project/study. Compensation is also determined by whether the research role is part of another position (e.g., faculty member, graduate or teaching assistant) or if the individual is hired independently as a researcher, research associate, or research assistant. Some positions may be part-time and/or combined with other positions and some positions may wage-based.

Workplace(s): These include independent or governmental research institutes, centers, or groups; academic departments; and academic or independent gerontology institutes and centers. Some opportunities exist for research consultants with doctoral degrees.

Employment Outlook: Good—but dependent on funding by government, institutions, foundations, and other funding sources.

Related Professional Organizations and Web Sites:
- Gerontology Research Center, National Institute on Aging (NIA): www.grc.nia.nih.gov
- Gerontological Society of America (GSA): www.geron.org
- American Statistical Association: www.amstat.org
- Discipline/Profession-based professional organizations with research focus, such as:
  - American Psychological Association (APA): www.apa.org
  - American Sociological Association (ASA): www.asanet.org

An Interview with Abbe Linscott, Research Associate, University-Based Gerontology Center

What is your educational background in gerontology and other disciplines or professional fields? What formal credentials (e.g., completed degrees, certification) do you hold in these fields?

I have a Bachelor of Arts degree in Sociology, with a management minor (May, 2003), and a Master of Gerontological Studies degree (May, 2006).

Briefly describe your gerontology-related career path.

I have always enjoyed being around older people since I was a child, but my first experience of working in the field came during my senior year in high school. I had an internship with an occupational therapist at a local nursing facility where I worked one-on-one with older adults. Because that was a successful experience, I decided to pursue a degree in occupational therapy (OT). I switched majors after realizing it was not the medical side I was interested in, but rather the social, personal side of OT that I enjoyed. I volunteered and had an internship with aging-related organizations (Alzheimer's Association and a local dialysis lab) while I was in college. The chair of the sociology department at my undergraduate university informed me of the Master of Gerontological Studies program at a nearby university. After taking a year off, I applied and was accepted into this graduate program. During my graduate studies in gerontology, I became very interested in policies and programs related to the aging population, so between my first and second year of graduate school, I had an internship in Washington DC with the National Council on Aging's (NCOA) Access to Benefits Coalition. Following graduation, I worked briefly with MyMedicareMatters, educating Medicare beneficiaries about the prescription drug program, and then I worked as a service coordinator in a senior housing facility, where I connected elders to resources in the community. Following this position, I interviewed for my current position as a research associate with a university-based gerontology center.

How did you first become interested in your current professional position?

I first became interested in my current professional position while I was a service coordinator with my previous job. As a service coordinator, I was at the grassroots level and working one-on-one with older adults. While I do enjoy working one-on-one with older adults, I realized that I missed being in the world of academia and the opportunity to constantly be learning. I was informed of the position I currently hold and knew it would be a perfect fit. I would be in an environment that fostered learning while producing work at the same time that could have a positive impact on the lives of older adults.

What are the most rewarding aspects of your career?

Watching a project I am managing through all of its stages, from the very earliest stages to its completion, and knowing that in the end, it will go towards improving the lives of older adults. Always learning something new! This is a position where there is constant change. I am never bored and I have new challenges every day. Being in an environment where everyone I work with shares my passion for producing high-quality, useful, and important work.

What are the most challenging aspects of your career?

I am not sure if it is so much of a challenge now, but, in the beginning, I really had to adjust to the constant change that takes place here. I had to realize that schedules and timelines do not always work out the way I hoped or thought they would and I needed to learn how to adjust so that I would be ready for changes when they occurred.

Describe a typical workday in your current professional position.

The research associate position is one that changes every day, so it is hard to describe exactly what a typical day looks like. Usually, though, once I'm in the office, I check all my voicemail and e-mail messages and respond to messages that need my immediate attention. The rest of the day depends on what part of our larger project I am working on. Sometimes I review manuals, update a survey we are working on, talk with key informants, meet with other colleagues to go over the aspects of the project, have conference calls with our national partners, or complete paperwork, such as an Institutional Review Board (IRB) application, to continue the research process. I know I will have different tasks once we have moved on to different stages of our project. For example, I will be involved in data gathering, analysis and report writing further down the line. Again, it varies from day-to-day, so there is not usually a 'typical' part of the day other than I am in the same place.

How do you balance career and other aspects of your life?

I am someone who very much values the time I have with my family and friends and I really work to make sure there is a very fair balance. I have always been a person who works very hard during the times that I am at work, so I am able to spend quality time with my family and friends. I have established more of an unwritten rule with myself that once I leave the office, I am finished with work until I return the next day. This does not mean that I will not think about a few work-related issues I need to address, but I will not actually address them until I am back in the office. I strongly believe that if you work hard and efficiently during the time you are at work, then this balance between work life and home life is not difficult to obtain.

What advice do you have for someone contemplating a career in gerontology? In a professional position similar to your current position?

I would strongly encourage anyone to consider a career in gerontology. This is a wonderful, not to mention, growing field, which provides many opportunities. Due to the multidisciplinary nature of gerontology, a person in this field is equipped to work in a variety of different positions. My advice would be to be very open-minded as to where you can go and the jobs you can find in the field of gerontology. My advice for someone contemplating a position as a research associate would be to be flexible, open to change and revision, and willing to work closely with a diverse team of colleagues.

Senior Companion Program (SCP) Director
Senior Companion Program (SCP) Coordinator

Basic Description: The Senior Companion Program (SCP) is a Senior Corps program affiliated with the Corporation for National and Community Service. Through SCP, persons 60 years of age and older assist and support other older persons to continue living independently in their own homes and communities. **SCP Directors** manage the overall operation of the program, including the following tasks: develop and monitor program budget; write, monitor, and manage grants; supervise paid staff (SCP Coordinators and clerical staff); identify volunteer stations that fit SCP guidelines and meet community needs in the program's service area; recruit, train, place, and evaluate volunteers (the Senior Companions); and maintain open communication with and respond to issues, concerns, and problems that arise among program staff, volunteers, and volunteer station personnel (see Mooradian interview). **SCP Coordinators** work directly with Senior Companions on a daily basis and assist the SCP director with budget and grant preparation; volunteer recruitment, training, and evaluation; maintain required schedule, volunteer hours, performance, and other records for individual volunteers; and other tasks as requested by the director.

Educational and Experience Requirements: SCP Director requires a minimum of a bachelor's degree in related field (e.g., human development, psychology, family studies, social work). Graduate degree work is required by some employing agencies, and coursework or a degree component in gerontology, program management, or volunteer agency administration is desirable. A minimum of 5–7 years of work experience in a human services related field is also essential. **SCP Coordinator** requires a bachelor's degree in a related field (e.g., human development, psychology, family studies, social work). Coursework or a degree component in gerontology is encouraged.

Certification, Licensure, and Continuing Education Requirements:
Professionals must meet all state licensure requirements related to the base
professional field, and continuing education requirements may be specified by
employing agency or program mandates.

Core Competencies and Skills Needed:
- Firm knowledge of state and federal policies, guidelines, and procedures
  for SCP
- Good organizational skills
- Good time and budget management skills
- Good volunteer supervision skills
- Knowledge of peer counseling techniques
- Comfortable with working in disadvantaged communities or community
  settings
- Good interpersonal communication skills
- Grant writing skills

Compensation: This varies by one's education, experience, type and level of
position, the nature of the employing agency, and the geographical location.
The position may be part-time or combined with another part-time position,
such as directing or coordinating another older adult volunteer program or
doing case/care management.

Workplace(s): This is usually with the county commission on aging or
another aging-specific human service agency; Senior Companions are placed
with "clients" who are homebound, reside in long-term care facilities, or participate in adult day care programs, and other relevant settings.

Employment Outlook: Moderate—but contingent upon continued SCP funding.

Related Professional Organizations and Web Sites:
- Corporation for National and Community Service: www.cns.gov

---

Speech-Language Pathologist

Basic Description: Speech-language pathologists work with all aspects of
human communication and communication disorders, including the evaluation, diagnosis, and treatment of speech, language, cognitive-communication,

and swallowing disorders. Although some speech-language pathologists work in multi-age work settings, many work in settings in which their clients and patients are predominantly older persons. In addition to providing evaluation, diagnostic, and treatment services, speech-language pathologists may: engage in research to enhance knowledge about normal human communication processes or disorders, and/or identify new strategies for treating communication disorders; develop new evaluation or treatment methods and products; supervise or direct clinical programs; manage private practices, clinics, agencies, or organizations; or teach in college/university speech-language academic programs. Speech-language pathologists who work with older adult patients frequently work as a member of an interdisciplinary health care team. Some speech-language pathologists also hold credentials and practice as audiologists (see Audiologist).

Education and Experience Requirements: This position requires a minimum of a bachelor's degree in communication sciences and disorders. Graduate-level education is required for clinical practice and a PhD is required for teaching, research, and private practice.

Certification, Licensure, and Continuing Education Requirements: Speech-language pathologists must comply with regulatory (licensure) standards in the state(s) where the practice occurs. Individuals who hold a graduate degree in speech-language pathology are eligible for the Certificate of Clinical Competence in Speech-Language Pathology (CCC-SLP), which is issued by the Council for Clinical Certification (CFCC) of the American Speech-Language-Hearing Association (ASHA). Requirements include a graduate degree in speech-language pathology earned through an academic program accredited by the Council on Academic Accreditation in Audiology and Speech-Language Pathology (CAA), a supervised clinical fellowship (CF), and a passing score on a national examination.

Core Competencies and Skills Needed: ASHA-identified requirements include:
- Sincere interest in helping people
- Above average intellectual aptitude and scientific aptitude adequate for the field
- Sensitivity, personal warmth, and perspective to interact with persons dealing with a communication disorder
- Patience, tolerance, persistence
- Emotional stability
- Resourcefulness and imagination
- Commitment to work cooperatively with others
- Effective oral and written communication skills

Compensation: This varies by one's education, experience, specialty, type of work setting, and the geographical location.

Workplace(s): These include hospitals/medical centers, rehabilitation centers, short-term and long-term nursing care facilities, community clinics, private practice offices, state and local health departments, state and federal agencies, home care/home health care agencies, adult day care programs/centers, research laboratories, and college/university academic departments and training labs.

Employment Outlook: Excellent—faster than average growth is expected through 2014 due to the rapid growth of the older adult population; an anticipated increase in incidences of neurological disorders with associated speech, language, swallowing, and hearing impairments; medical advances that are improving the survival rate of trauma and stroke victims; and the increased used of contract services by hospitals/medical centers, long-term and nursing care facilities.

Related Professional Organizations and Web Sites:
- American Speech-Language-Hearing Association (ASHA): www.asha.org
- Informal Interest Group on Language and Communication, Gerontological Society of America (GSA): www.geron.org

---

State Health Insurance Counseling and Assistance Program (SHIP) Coordinator

Basic Description: The State Health Insurance Counseling and Assistance Program (SHIP) is a free health-benefits counseling service funded by federal and state governments (independent of the for-profit insurance industry) for Medicare and Medicaid recipients and their families or caregivers. The goal of the program is to educate, advocate, and counsel these persons so they become empowered to make informed and appropriate decisions and choices related to the programs for which they are eligible. SHIP Coordinators work directly with clients. They also recruit, guide, direct, and supervise SHIP Counselors (volunteers). Specific types of assistance and counseling addressed through SHIP include: billing concerns; evaluation and comparison of long-term care and supplemental ("Medigap") insurance policies; Medicaid assistance, including preparation of applications;

Medicare appeals; prescription drug assistance programs; managed care (Medicare Advantage) options; and suspected waste, fraud, and abuse. SHIP coordinators network with other local aging services and community groups. In some states, SHIP goes by an alternative name, such as the Michigan Medicare/Medicaid Assistance Program (MMAP).

Education and Experience Requirements: This position requires a minimum of a Bachelor's in Social Work (BSW) degree. Gerontology coursework, a degree component, or a certificate is recommended.

Certification, Licensure, and Continuing Education Requirements: SHIP coordinators must comply with appropriate state licensure requirements for their base profession. They must complete an initial 4-day SHIP training program and attend two refresher training sessions each year.

Core Competencies and Skills Needed:
- Willingness to learn about health insurance provisions and claims filing issues; ability to retain learned information
- Good working knowledge of Medicaid and Medicare programs, insurance industry products, especially long-term care and supplemental insurance policies, prescription assistance programs, and related issues
- Good organizational skills
- Advocacy skills
- Good communication (oral, written, and listening) skills
- Good interpersonal skills
- Ability to manage, lead, and support volunteers
- Patience; sensitive and caring attitude
- Willingness to tackle special problems and follow through to resolution

Compensation: This varies by one's educational and experience background, the type of employing agency, and the geographical location.

Workplace(s): These include Area Agencies on Aging, county departments/commissions on aging, senior service agencies, and similar agencies/organizations. Travel to offsite work locations is usually necessary.

Employment Outlook: Moderate—but contingent upon continued SHIP funding.

Related Professional Organizations and Web Sites:
- Listing of SHIP contact information for all states: www.medicare.gov/contacts/static/allStateContacts.asp
- Web site for SHIP in a specific state, for example, Michigan Medicare/Medicaid Assistance Program (MMAP): www.mymapp.org

An Interview with
Sarah Kusnier,
MMAP (SHIP) Coordinator,
County Commission on Aging

What is your educational background in gerontology and other disciplines or professional fields? What formal credentials (e.g., completed degrees, certification) do you hold in these fields?

I earned a Bachelor's of Social Work degree with a minor in sociology. Also, I completed the Michigan Medicare Assistance Program (MMAP) training for MMAP counselors, then for MMAP coordinators. For both positions there is an initial four-day training program, plus a minimum of two refresher trainings per year.

Briefly describe your gerontology-related career path.

As an undergraduate, I took a couple of gerontology courses, but it wasn't my minor. One gerontology course focused on activities to do with older adults who have various diseases (Alzheimer's disease and other dementias, for example), while another course focused on health and physical issues. These courses enabled me to understand the aging process and signs to look for in various diseases. This is my first position working with elders. During my undergraduate internship at the commission on aging, I worked mainly with the MMAP coordinator who was there at the time. When my internship ended, she retired and I had the opportunity to apply for the position. From there, I went through more training to become the coordinator.

How did you first become interested in your current professional position?

For an undergraduate gerontology course, I had to do a project that required me to spend a set number of volunteer hours in a nursing home. The types of activities I participated in at the nursing home included one-on-one visits with the patients, assisting with the board and game hour in the activity room, and helping with other activities such as picnics. The assignment was to focus on one individual and to evaluate him or her, throughout the weeks, for any cognitive or physical changes. Through this volunteer work, I realized that older adults are very interesting and have many experiences to share. For the most part, they also seem to be very appreciative of the little things that you do for them. Also, I have been close to my grandparents as I've grown up and I believe that has had some influence.

What are the most rewarding aspects of your career?

I work a lot with Medicare D (prescription drug plan) and when I hear a client say, "I didn't know how I was going to afford my medications till you helped me out," it is this kind of statement that makes me keep going. To me, our older clients are very appreciative individuals and when they say a simple thank you, I find that very rewarding.

What are the most challenging aspects of your career?

Regulations. It is frustrating when I want to help someone, but they are ineligible because of the mandatory income/asset limits or other restrictions in a particular regulation. Some clients earn too much to get the extra help, even when they are struggling with nonmedical bills (for example, house and car payments, home insurance, daily living expenses) and this leaves them with not enough left over to pay for the required amount for Medicare D to help cover the cost of multiple medical prescriptions. I find that many of my clients do struggle to qualify and that's another challenge, because there is only so much we can do through commission on aging and MMAP services and programs. Another challenging aspect is getting familiar with all the insurance companies. In the county where I work, for example, there are more than 50 Medicare D plans and 10 or more Medicare Advantage plans. Then, add in all of the companies that offer "medigap" plans. All of this information can be overwhelming to absorb well enough to give my clients adequate and accurate information and counseling.

Describe a typical workday in your current professional position.

It really depends on the time of the year. The open enrollment for Medicare D is November 15–December 31 of every year and, during this time, it is very busy. It's usually one client after another. I am thankful, though, that I do have volunteer counselors who also have been through MMAP training. During the rest of the year, it's a steadier pace. I mainly assist those who are new to Medicare and those who are dual eligible (that is, they have both Medicare and Medicaid). Throughout the year, I also assist clients dealing with insurance fraud or incorrect billings or claims. In a typical day, though, I work with clients by searching for and reviewing Medicare D plans, "medigap" plans, Medicare Advantage plans, and Medicaid applications.

How do you balance career and other aspects of your life?

I have a sign in my office that states, "Don't confuse having a career with having a life." I try to follow that advice. I try to keep my work at work and my outside life outside of work. If I go home stressed out by work, it will affect my relationship with my family and friends and I don't want to do that. Yes, there are days that I do go home stressed out, but my family understands and they are there to hear me vent, then I'll be okay from there. I know that I will have my bad days, but I also know that more good days do happen and, often, they do outweigh the bad days.

What advice do you have for someone contemplating a career in gerontology? In a professional position similar to your current position?

In a gerontology-related career, one must keep in mind the need to be patient. Older clients can take longer to make decisions and to perform the daily tasks, like walking and getting their words out, but some of this is part of growing older. Some, however, are just confused by how complex these new plans and options are. For someone who is contemplating on becoming a SHIP/MMAP counselor or coordinator, you must be able to deal with the ups and downs. You will have good days and bad days. You are going to be working with clients who can afford Medicare D and their prescriptions and with others who just can't make ends meet. Also, you can't always solve a problem or resolve the issue; there are going to be days when you can try your hardest, but still that person can't be fully helped. Keep in mind that you can't really change the system—you have to learn how to work within the limitations of the system.

Strategic Policy Advisor
Strategic Policy Analyst

Basic Description: Strategic policy advisors and analysts identify emerging policy issues, propose and advocate for policy legislation and regulations that fit organizational mission and goals, monitor relevant proposed legislation, and keep organizational peers and constituents apprised of relevant policy actions. They serve as resource persons for professional peers within the organization and represent the organization in external interactive or collaborative policy efforts with legislative/regulatory bodies and other organizations/agencies. They may conduct or oversee original research related to policy issues of concern; prepare, review, and/or provide oversight for reports and organizational publications; and make presentations at press conferences and professional meetings or for boards, technical/advisory panels, and commissions.

Education and Experience Requirements: This profession requires a master's or doctoral degree in public policy, political science, social sciences, law, or closely related field, with the doctorate preferred. Gerontology coursework or a degree component is strongly recommended and 5 or more years of directly related policy experience is usually required.

Certification, Licensure, and Continuing Education Requirements: None is required.

Core Competencies and Skills Needed:
- Excellent working knowledge of the processes of advocacy and policy development/enactment
- Technical knowledge of federal and state legislative processes related to older adult needs, issues, and concerns
- Specific knowledge related to the focus of the employing agency or specific agency program (e.g., health, financial security, housing, long-term care, grandparent caregiving or visitation)
- Knowledge of research methodologies related to the identified focus for a specific career position
- Excellent written and oral communication skills
- Excellent interpersonal skills

- Excellent presentation skills; capable of presenting subject matter information to various types of audiences
- Ability to persuade peers of the merits of proposed policy and relevance to organizational goals
- Ability to objectively analyze and critique proposed legislation and regulations of relevance

Compensation: This varies by one's education, experience, level of responsibility, the nature of the employment setting, and the geographical location.

Workplace(s): These include national advocacy organizations, legislative staff positions (including campaign staff), lobbying organizations, and professional organizations.

Employment Outlook: Good potential—but may be limited due to budget restrictions and lack of broader recognition of the need for and value of policy professionals with gerontology expertise.

Related Professional Organizations and Web Sites:
- American Political Science Association (APSA): www.apsanet.org
- AARP: www.aarp.org

Technical Assistance Specialist, National-Level Transportation Center

Basic Description: The Technical Assistance Specialist participates in site visits to assess local/state transportation options, gathers information on transportation options available to older adults, identifies gaps in services, and prepares site visit reports; assists in preparing for meetings by producing meeting materials and preparing PowerPoint presentations; represents the Center and assists Center administrators at conferences and events by developing Center marketing materials, staffing exhibit booths, and disseminating materials; responds to requests for technical assistance that arrive through the Center's toll-free information line and Web site inquiries; understands and endorses the Center's mission and values, as well as the sponsoring agency's strategic priorities; and performs other duties as assigned or requested by the Center administrator.

Education and Experience Requirements: This position requires a bachelor's degree in business, human or social services, or a related field and 3–5 years of relevant experience.

Certification, Licensure, and Continuing Education Requirements: A valid driver's license is required.

Core Competencies and Skills Needed:
- Knowledge of formal aging network
- Knowledge of human service transportation
- Ability to provide technical assistance to diverse groups
- Ability to research transportation programs and technical assistance tools
- Ability to work with multiple team partners
- Excellent computer skills, including word processing, technical software, and use of the Internet
- Excellent written and verbal communication skills
- Ability to juggle multiple priorities and ability to multitask
- Excellent customer service skills
- Good organizational and time management skills
- Ability to work both independently and collaboratively
- Availability to travel for work

Compensation: This depends on one's education, amount and type of experience, and level of technical skills.

Workplace(s): These include the center headquarters and other relevant worksites.

Employment Outlook: Limited—to only one position per center, but the creation of additional centers and programs with similar mission and goals should provide additional opportunities. Similar positions may be available with community- and state-based programs on transportation for elders or with general transportation systems interested in meeting the transportation needs of older adults.

Related Professional Organizations and Web Sites:
- National Highway Transportation Safety Administration (NHTSA): www.nhtsa.dot.gov
- American Medical Association (AMA)'s Older Drivers Project: www.ama-assn.org/go/olderdrivers
- Formal Interest Group on Transportation and Aging, Gerontological Society of America (GSA): www.geron.org

Volunteer Program Coordinator

Basic Description: Volunteer program coordinators recruit, train, supervise, and evaluate individuals who provide volunteer services to or on behalf of their organization, agency, or facility. They solicit volunteer worksites, serve as the liaison with staff members and clients at the volunteer site, match volunteers with worksites, keep records of volunteer schedules and hours, provide ongoing support for their volunteers, organize award ceremonies to honor outstanding volunteers, and keep their own supervisors and colleagues apprised of volunteer activity. This position may require considerable travel time to potential and actual volunteer worksites and offsite locations where work-related meetings, training sessions, and events are held.

Education and Experience Requirements: This position requires a minimum of an associate's or bachelor's degree in a relevant field. Prior experience as a volunteer and with volunteer programs is strongly recommended, as is gerontology coursework or a degree component and prior experience working with older adults. Coursework, seminars, and/or training sessions on interpersonal communication skills, time management, and working with diverse populations are encouraged.

Certification, Licensure, and Continuing Education Requirements: Certification in Volunteer Administration (CVA) is an increasing preference of employers. Participation in organizations and conferences for volunteer managers is encouraged.

Core Competencies and Skills Needed:
- Good time management skills
- Good organizational skills and the ability to stay organized
- Good interpersonal communication skills
- Good people management skills
- Computer and technology proficiency
- Base knowledge of volunteer management
- Need to stay current with volunteerism issues and trends
- Knowledge of new initiative on Civic Engagement in an Older America
- Ability to work with diverse groups of people
- Patience

Compensation: This varies by one's education, experience, the nature of the employing agency, level of position, and the geographical location. The position may be part-time or combined with responsibility for another program or service.

Workplace(s): These include agencies and organizations that serve elders (for example, Area Agencies on Aging, county departments/commissions on aging, AARP), medical and long-term care centers, and arts and humanities organizations that rely on older volunteers (for example, community art, music, and theatre organizations; museums).

Employment Outlook: Excellent—due to the trend toward the civic engagement of older persons.

Related Professional Organizations and Web Sites:
- Congress of Volunteer Administrators Association (CVAA): www.covaa.org
- State and regional volunteer managers and administrators organizations, such as the Northwest Oregon Volunteer Administrators Association: www.novaa.org
- National Academy on an Aging Society (NAAS): www.agingsociety.org (for information on Civic Engagement in an Older America)

An Interview with Gretchen S. Jordan, Volunteer Resources Manager/ Program Coordinator

What is your educational background in gerontology and other disciplines or professional fields? What formal credentials (e.g., completed degrees, certification) do you hold in these fields?

I am currently enrolled in online classes to earn my Bachelor's degree in Human and Community Services from an out-of-state university. I have a General Education associate's degree from a local community college. Previous coursework includes courses on management, aging and society, diversity and training. I earned Certification in Volunteer Administration (CVA) in 2004 from the Association of Volunteer Administrators (AVA). Although AVA no longer exists, the CVA certification program is still available through the Council on Certification for Volunteer Administration.

Briefly describe your gerontology-related career path.

I spent 15+ years as a McDonald's manager, where I was responsible for recruiting, interviewing, hiring, training and supervising older workers. After leaving the corporate world, I spent 10 years in nonprofit work with the local council for Camp Fire USA. During this time, I also worked for two years with a teen parent program, where I supervised older volunteers who mentored unwed mothers, provided childcare and donated services/supplies to clients and the program. From there, I became the program coordinator for a child care and resource referral, where many of the childcare providers were elders. From 1996 to 2004, I was the program manager of a club program and many of the volunteers I worked with were alumni of Camp Fire. Since coming to my current position with AARP in 2004, I have had many opportunities to increase my knowledge of the gerontology field through AARP's print and online resources. Direct collaboration with some of our statewide partners, such as senior centers, Retired Senior Volunteers Program (RSVP), and Area Agencies on Aging (AAA), has given me opportunities for practical application of what I have learned.

How did you first become interested in your current professional position?

I started as a volunteer myself and many experiences as a volunteer for a youth service agency led me to a paid position using my people and management skills to manage programs and volunteers for that agency. I was looking for an opportunity to work for another nonprofit organization—one with a mission that was relevant to me personally and professionally. About the same time, AARP saw a clear need to increase staffing in its state offices to provide for a person with specific skills in working with older volunteers and made the commitment to hire a staff member whose main job function was to recruit, train, and manage volunteers, programs that use volunteers, and fellow staff members who work with volunteers within the organization. When this position opened, I applied for it and was hired.

What are the most rewarding aspects of your career?

The people! I find older volunteers to be very competent, willing to learn, and honest about their abilities and desires. What I have learned from my volunteers about their career and life experiences has enabled me to use this knowledge to improve the programs and systems in my job, as well as giving me a sincere feeling of fulfillment and ability to positively embrace aging for myself and my family. While I am somewhat younger than most of the people I work with, it's not a feeling of working with my parents or grandparents, rather more like working with mentors and competent elders.

What are the most challenging aspects of your career?

More than half of the volunteers I work with are still employed, so there are challenges with these volunteers' availability. If there are medical or caregiving issues, of course, those take precedent over their volunteer duties. Usually, the biggest challenge is scheduling volunteers for activities and programs. They do tend to put their personal and retirement activities first, which is totally understandable and part of the 'territory,' so communication is very important. At times, I find that older volunteers aren't able to react quickly and need more time to be informed or trained for a specific task or issue. Also, when volunteers have strong negative feelings about an issue, they have the option to not volunteer for that issue.

Describe a typical workday in your current professional position.

First hour: check emails, return phone calls, check in with coworkers and supervisor. Second hour: call volunteers for interviews, schedule trainings, make volunteer follow up calls, request volunteers to help with projects/events for fellow staff. Third hour: work on projects, meet with volunteers who have specific volunteer roles (such as scheduling other volunteers for health fairs and informational fairs). Fourth hour: meet with staff to plan projects, follow up on current events and similar tasks. Fifth hour: lunch break or take a volunteer to lunch. Sixth hour: read online or print documents about volunteerism issues. Seventh hour: continue working on project and volunteer issues. Eighth hour and beyond: follow up on phone calls, e-mail, and other duties or projects that may have come up during the day, prepare for the next day's events or meetings. Evening: attend meeting(s) for a professional volunteer managers' association I belong to.

How do you balance career and other aspects of your life?

I become the volunteer to keep my perspective fresh and try to involve my family along with me. If I have meetings, trainings or events away from the office, I try to schedule them so it's not as disruptive to the family (for example, do these in one longer period rather than several small ones). A sense of humor is important because some times I just can't escape the aging issues I work with every day. After all, I am aging and I do have caregiving duties for my parents and in-laws. Most of my friends and colleagues know I work for AARP and it's a well respected organization, so I do find myself remaining attached in some way to work even if it is just answering questions or offering to send materials. I am lucky to have a supervisor who recognizes the need for "down time" after a long day or an intense project, so I do have the option to be flexible with my schedule. If there are extended trips, family is welcome to accompany me if I pay for their expenses.

What advice do you have for someone contemplating a career in gerontology? In a professional position similar to your current position?

I think a career in gerontology, especially working with volunteers, has a strong future with good possibilities for growth and advancement. The changing demographics of the American population ensure many varied and interesting career choices. Take classes in fields that interest you, especially ones that may help you improve your people and communication skills. Computer and updated skills on contemporary technology will be very helpful. When working with volunteers, have a strong understanding of how the nonprofit works, as well as a good knowledge of human resources. Most of the time, your job managing volunteers will include organizational development, training and program coordination, so management, event planning, and public speaking experience will be job skills that you use every day. I also encourage someone with more than three years of volunteer management experience to obtain Certification in Volunteer Administration (CVA designation).

. . . and More

An increasing number of job postings related to aging and work with or on behalf of older adults are seeking applicants with a background that includes gerontology education and work experience. More college graduates, at all levels, have completed at least some gerontology coursework, and many have formal credentials in the form of minors, majors, cognates, specializations, certificates, and degrees. More disciplines and professional fields are adding gerontology to programs of study for their undergraduate and graduate students. More college graduates have had an intergenerational service learning experience or completed a gerontology-related internship, practicum, or fieldwork. As a result, there is a bigger menu of gerontology options from which to choose if you are selecting an undergraduate major or minor, making decisions about graduate study, making a career transition, or trying to find your niche in the professional world.

In addition to the career path and positions presented in the previous profiles and interviews, here are even more options for you to consider. The information provided includes the specific discipline or professional field, suggestions about existing and potential positions, and, when available, relevant professional organizations and Web sites. For all of these options, it is assumed that academic preparation for the positions listed would include gerontology coursework or a gerontology degree component. Keep in mind that many of the suggested paths and positions are just beginning to emerge or have not yet been explored.

ACCOUNTING

Although gerontology is not part of the academic education of accountants, many do have older adult clients and some handle quite complex accounting situations with their elderly clients. Certificate and registry programs for business and financial professionals, however, are opening the door for accountants to focus their practice more visibly on accounting and financial planning services for elders. Possible professional positions for persons with a combined accounting and gerontology background include:

- Tax advisor for older clients
- Certified Senior Advisor (CSA)

- Certified Financial Planner (CFP)
- Registered Financial Gerontology (RFG)

Relevant professional organizations and Web sites:

- The American Institute of Certified Public Accountants (AICPA): www.aicpa.org
- Society of Certified Senior Advisors: www.society-csa.com
- Certified Financial Planner Board of Standards, Inc.: www.cfp.net
- American Institute of Financial Gerontology (AIFG): www.aifg.org

ADVERTISING

With the growing population of elders and a wider array of products and services being designed to meet the needs of elders across the continuum from well and active, to frail and disabled, there is a parallel need for advertising professionals to have a broader and more accurate education about aging processes, interests and needs of elders, and the considerable diversity of this population group. Possible positions for persons with a combined background in advertising and gerontology include:

- Account executive for products for older adults
- Ad writer
- Director of advertising for a publication aimed at older adults

Relevant professional organizations and Web sites:

- American Advertising Federation (AAF): www.aaf.org
- Ad Council: www.adcouncil.org
- American Association of Advertising Agencies (AAAA): www.aaaa.org

ANTHROPOLOGY

There is a relatively small but steady group of academic researchers and educators, especially in the subfields of cultural and medical anthropology, whose teaching and research focuses on aging. Recently, there also appears to be some movement toward the creation of applied or clinical practice opportunities for persons with bachelor's and master's degrees in anthropology who are interested in aging. Possible professional positions for persons with a combined anthropology and gerontology background include:

- Ethnographer
- Consultant on aging for community-based cultural affairs programs
- Trainer on culturally competent professional practice with older adults, their families, and caregivers

Relevant professional organizations and Web sites:

- American Anthropological Association (AAA): www.aanet.org
- Association for Anthropology and Gerontology (AAGE) [Check www. aaanet.org for possible further information]
- Society for Applied Anthropology (SfAA): www.sfaa.net
- Network of Multicultural Aging (NOMA), American Society on Aging (NOMA): www.asaging.org
- Informal Interest Group on International Aging and Migration, Gerontological Society of America (GSA): www.geron.org

BANKING

Changes in banking processes and in the aging population jointly create new opportunities for banking officials to devise new and appropriate ways to market their services to older persons, and to educate their elderly clients about new banking products and processes. Possible professional positions for persons with a combined banking and gerontology background include:

- Older adult customer service representative
- Trust officer
- Reverse mortgage specialist
- Educational consultant to train bankers about aging and older adult service needs
- Consultant on aging to marketing division of a banking corporation

Relevant professional organizations and Web sites:

- American Bankers Association (ABA): www.aba.com

CLOTHING AND TEXTILES

Except for some attention to the need for adaptive clothing for persons of all ages who are physically disabled, the clothing and textiles industry has been slow to respond to the desire of older consumers for clothing, household textiles, and textile-based furnishings that are attractive and stylish, yet also accommodate normal physical changes in human bodies. It also seems necessary to develop education/training about aging for clothing designers, buyers, and sales/store personnel. Possible professional positions for individuals who combine the study of clothing and textiles with gerontology include:

- Custom clothiers
- Designer of clothing to meet the diverse needs and interests of older adults along the functional continuum from active and well to frail and disabled
- Trainer on aging for retail clothing sales personnel
- Freelance personal shopper for older clients
- Gerontology consultant to designers and buyers
- In-store consumer representative for older clients
- Clothing and textiles instructor
- Buyer of textiles products for older adult residences or long-term care facilities
- Consultant on aging for a fabric manufacturer
- Costume designer for a senior theatre company

Relevant professional organizations and Web sites:

- Professional Association of Custom Clothiers (PPAC): www.paccprofessionals.org
- American Association of Family and Consumer Sciences (AAFCS): www.aafcs.org

CREATIVE WRITING

While a career as a creative writer does not require a college degree, there seems to be an explosion of creative writing programs, especially master's in fine arts (MFA) degree programs in creative writing. It is not clear if any of these degree programs have linkages with the gerontology programs on their campuses, but such a linkage could be very fruitful for persons interested in writing about aging in any genre. Possible professional positions for persons with a combined creative writing and gerontology background include:

- Screenwriter
- Playwright
- Essayist

- Novel author
- Creative nonfiction writer
- Short story author
- Memoirist
- Biographer or autobiographer
- Greeting card writer
- Freelance writer for magazines
- Acquisitions editor for books on aging for a publisher
- Copyeditor for writings on aging
- Consultant on aging for writers, writing programs, and writer's retreats

Relevant professional organizations and Web sites:

- Association of Writers and Writing Programs (AWP): www.awpwriter.org
- Modern Language Association (MLA): www.mla.org

EDUCATIONAL GERONTOLOGY

In addition to positions for curriculum on aging developers/teachers in K-12 school systems and gerontology professors and program administrators in higher education, opportunities exist for other professionals with combined backgrounds in education and gerontology, such as:

- Administrators, teachers, curriculum developers, and program coordinators with Elderhostel, Elderhostel's network of Institutes for Learning in Retirement, and other participative learning experiences for older persons
- Curriculum developer on aging for corporate and industry professionals
- Coordinator of an older learner program for a senior center
- College/university professor of adult education or educational gerontology
- Coordinator of a campus-based initiative, program, or center to involve older adults in campus life (as students, mentors, and in other roles)
- Curriculum designer of training seminars and workshops for Alzheimer's Association or similar organizations

Relevant professional organizations, resources, and Web sites:

- Association for Gerontology in Higher Education (AGHE): www.aghe.org
- Lifetime Education and Renewal Network (LEARN), American Society on Aging (ASA): www.asaging.org

ELDER ABUSE, NEGLECT, AND EXPLOITATION

Attention to the various forms of elder abuse has been gained through media coverage, the development of interagency coalitions to raise awareness about and decrease the incidence of elder abuse, and governmental funding at state and federal levels for initiatives to prevent elder abuse, neglect, and exploitation. Professionals from quite a few backgrounds (such as family studies, marriage and family therapy, social gerontology, sociology/applied sociology, law and law enforcement, social work, geriatric medicine, gerontological nursing) are involved in these efforts. Possible professional positions related to one or more aspects of elder abuse include:

- Adult/older adult protective services caseworker
- Consumer fraud prevention educator for elders
- Support program coordinator for older adult victims of abuse, neglect, or exploitation
- Law enforcement officer who specializes in elder abuse, neglect, and/or exploitation
- Team leader for a collaborative community consortium to prevent elder abuse, neglect, and exploitation
- Counselor/therapist for family and caregiving abusers of elders
- Domestic violence counselor or therapist family practice with elders and their families
- Consultant on sexual abuse of elders

Relevant professional organizations and Web sites:

- National Center on Elder Abuse (NCEA): www.elderabusecenter.org
- Informal Interest Group on Abuse, Neglect and Exploitation of Elderly People, Gerontological Society of America (GSA): www.geron.org

ENTREPRENEURIAL GERONTOLOGY

Opportunities abound for gerontological specialists and gerontologists to develop products and deliver services for needs that are unmet or not yet met adequately through existing avenues. Simply put, an entrepreneur identifies one of these needs for a defined target audience, creates appropriate products or services to meet the need, designs an appropriate delivery system, and then delivers these products or services to the target audience. In fact, many gerontological specialists and gerontologists already carry out this process as part of their full-time positions when they deliver their knowledge through speaking engagements, training programs, and consultations with organizations, agencies, and facilities external to their regular employment setting. In these situations knowledge is their "product." In some cases, however, the "product" might be an item that they design or help to design or a service they provide. Many of the positions suggested in this . . . and More section offer entrepreneurial opportunities for gerontological specialists and gerontologists to combine their background in gerontology and in other fields (for example, as a personal clothier for older persons, exercise consultant for an in-home care agency, or freelance writer for newspapers or magazines). Here are a few more examples that currently exist or are possible:

- Interior designer turned relocation specialist, who assists older adult clients in making decisions about where to relocate, helps them decide which furnishings and other possessions will fit their new home, assists with distribution of excess furnishings and other possessions (e.g., through distribution to family members or friends, garage or yard sales, donations to charitable organizations, or consignment stores), coordinates selection and purchase of new furnishings and accessories for the new home, and helps older persons adapt to and get settled into the new living space
- Dietitian or nutrition educator turned personal food "trainer," who helps older adult clients adjust meal planning and food purchasing to meet changing dietary needs related to chronic health conditions and medication regimens; becomes personal shopper or shopping assistant for some clients
- Gerontology educator in higher education turned consultant on books about aging for independent bookstores and small town libraries, who assists with selection of fiction and nonfiction books on aging, creates displays that feature these books, facilitates a monthly discussion group on aging in literature, and recommends authors of books on aging to invite for a joint library-bookstore reading festival

Relevant professional organizations and Web sites:

- Consortium for Entrepreneurship Education, based at Ohio State University: www.entre-ed.org
- Several college/university colleges of business offer degrees or degree components in entrepreneurial studies and/or have centers or institutes for entrepreneurship

EXERCISE, FITNESS AND WELLNESS

Research findings indicate that older adults are increasing their involvement (voluntarily and through prescription) in exercise, fitness, and wellness activities via sport programs (such as Senior Olympics), fitness centers operated by medical centers or available in their retirement communities, and through privately owned fitness programs, wellness centers, and spas. Possible professional positions for persons with combined backgrounds in exercise physiology, physical education, therapeutic recreation or related fields, and gerontology include:

- Personal trainer for older adults
- Training coordinator for Senior Olympics
- Exercise consultant for in-home care agency
- Fitness specialist for a continuing care retirement community
- Lifestyle director for an active-adult facility
- Wellness director for a retirement community's wellness center
- Program coordinator for health club and spa that caters to elders

Relevant professional organizations and Web sites:

- American Alliance for Health, Physical Education, Recreation and Dance (AAHPERD): www.aahperd.org
- International Council on Active Aging (ICAA): www.icaa.cc

FAMILY GERONTOLOGY

Family gerontology is a newly emerging subfield of both gerontology and family studies (also known as family ecology, family relations, and family science), which is gaining visibility in academic coursework; professional journals, including a recently published issue of a National Council on Family Relations (NCFR) journal; scholarly books and trade books; and presentations at professional conferences in both fields. It is less visible, however, in regard to employment possibilities for graduates at the bachelor's and master's degree level. One factor in this may be that family gerontology, up to this point, has been based more in the realms of theory, research, and education at the college/university level than in practice and policy, which are more practitioner-oriented realms. Also, some of the most obvious positions for family gerontology practitioners are currently filled by social work graduates with BSW and MSW degrees. Another factor may be that family studies, as a professional practice field, has concentrated more on relationships and issues related to child and adolescent development and young families than on families in middle and later adulthood. If recent attention is a good indicator, however, it appears that the academic attention to family gerontology is beginning to open more doors for direct practice opportunities for family gerontological specialists. NCFR is currently surveying its members about the nature of their professional positions and the results may provide a clearer picture as to the type of gerontology-related positions currently held by family studies professionals. Professional positions that are or should be open to persons with a family gerontology background include:

- Coordinator of a Kinship Care project program or research project
- Family life educator for elders and their families
- Gerontological family specialist for hospice programs and facilities
- Marriage and therapist specializing in older adult relationships and concerns
- Family mediator specializing in elder care and kin care
- Adult Care Services vocational education instructor at the secondary school or community/junior college level
- Coordinator of family services, including support groups, for disease/ chronic condition-specific organizations (e.g., Alzheimer's disease, Parkinson's Disease, Arthritis, Type II Diabetes)

Relevant professional organizations and Web sites:

- National Council on Family Relations (NCFR): www.ncfr.org
- Informal Interest Group on Grandparents as Caregivers, Gerontological Society of America (GSA): www.geron.org
- American Association of Marriage and Family Therapy (AAMFT): www. aamft.org
- American Association of Family and Consumer Sciences (AAFCS): www. aafcs.org

FILM AND TELEVISION

Films (including documentary, educational, and feature-length films) and videotapes serve as key educational tools in gerontology education. AGHE has a brief bibliography, *Audiovisuals on Aging*, to assist gerontology educators in the selection of appropriate films for in the courses they teach. Film review sessions are offered by film distributors at the conferences of gerontology professional organizations. At each year's GSA annual scientific meeting, the Humanities and the Arts Committee shows a recently produced film on some aspect of aging; an open discussion with the filmmaker follows the viewing. Although many of these films are excellent, few are made by filmmakers who have a formal educational background in gerontology. Although there have been some feature-length films, made-for-TV movies, and television shows about aging with accurate portrayals of older adults, this is definitely a career path that needs further exploration. Possible professional positions for persons with a combined background in film and gerontology include:

- Faculty member in a school of film and/or television
- Gerontological consultant as a member of the filmmaking team
- Coach on aging for actors who play aging characters

For further information on education about and careers in film and television, contact related college/university department and professional school administrators and faculty.

HISTORY

History is another field in which the professionals with a gerontology background have been employed primarily in the academic ranks as history professors and/or researchers, although their numbers are quite limited. To encourage consideration of combining history and gerontology in a professional position, here are a few possible positions:

- Project director/coordinator for an oral history project related to aging/older adults
- Research writer on topics related to history of aging and field of gerontology
- History professor who specializes in history of aging and related topics

Relevant professional organizations and Web sites:

- American Historical Association (AHA): www.historians.org
- See *Careers for Students of History* online at AHA Web site

HOSPITALITY SERVICES AND TOURISM

As older adults turn more frequently to the hospitality and tourism industry to help them spend their leisure time, this is an industry with considerable potential for creation of gerontology-related professional positions, including the following:

- Gerontology consultant for hotel or restaurant chain
- Hospitality director/coordinator for a retirement community
- Staff trainer for hospitality services at a retirement community
- Director of travel for older adult organizations and active "senior living" residences
- Travel and tours coordinator for a county commission/division/bureau on aging
- Coordinator for a senior center or retirement community travel program
- Gerontology consultant to a travel industry organization or business, such as a bed & breakfast innkeepers association
- Director of grandparent-grandchild travel and education programs for an organization like Elderhostel or for theme parks
- Owner of a travel company that specializes in tours for older adults

Relevant professional organizations and Web sites:

- Business Forum on Aging (BFA), American Society on Aging (ASA): www.asaging.org
- Informal Interest Group on Business and Aging, Gerontological Society of America (GSA): www.geron.org
- For further information on education about and careers in hospitality services and tourism, consult related college/university departmental/program administrators and faculty

INTIMACY AND SEXUALITY/SEXUAL ORIENTATION/ SEXUAL HEALTH IN LATER LIFE

Yes, older adults can have sex, many do, and probably quite a few others find ways to maintain or rekindle intimacy and sexuality in their lives as they age. As gerontological specialists and gerontologists, it is possible to create supportive environments, provide social and emotional support, do appropriate research, and develop education and training programs—for elders, future and current professionals, caregivers, and others—in ways that support intimacy and sexual expression and sexual health for elders, regardless of age, gender, or sexual orientation. Possible professional positions, in addition to academic and professional school professors who teach courses on intimacy and sexuality in later life, sexual orientation, and sexual health, include:

- Intimacy and sexuality educators for older adult learner programs
- Program coordinator or counselor for programs serving lesbian, gay, bisexual, and transgender (LGBT) elders

- Program coordinator for program that serves parents/families of gay and lesbian elders
- HIV/AIDS educator or counselor for older adults
- Intimacy and sexuality counselors/therapists in medical and mental health clinics or private practice
- Sexuality and aging specialist for a county or state health department

Relevant professional organizations and Web sites:

- American Association of Sexuality Educators, Counselors and Therapists (AASECT): www.aasect.org
- Lesbian and Gay Aging Issues Network (LGAIN), American Society on Aging (ASA): www.asaging.org
- HIV, AIDS and Older Adults Informal Interest Group, Gerontological Society of America (GSA): www.geron.org

JOURNALISM, PUBLIC RELATIONS, AND COMMUNICATIONS

These three professional fields, sometime separate and sometimes combined in academic departments, offer a wide array of potential positions that could be enhanced by the integration of gerontology into one's program of study. One profiled position (see Communications Director, National Membership Organization) illustrates a job in which the staff member is responsible for tasks from each of these professional fields. Other positions, like those listed below, are more specific to one of the three fields:

- Newspaper columnist
- Editor for the Elder News page in city/community newspaper
- Freelance writer on aging for magazines and newspapers
- Newsletter editor for a community-based agency that serves elders
- Developer of online newsletter for older adults or professionals who work with older adults
- Public relations coordinator/director for a "senior living" residence or community
- Anchor of a news program on aging for television

Relevant professional organizations and Web sites:

- American Society of Journalists and Authors (ASJA): www.asja.org
- Society of Professional Journalists (SPJ): http://spj.org

- Association for Education in Journalism and Mass Communication (AEJMC): www.aejmc.org
- Public Relations Society of America: www.prsa.org

MARKETING

With the rapid expansion of the elderly population over the next two decades, the field of marketing may be one of the big winners in number and types of professional positions that will be enhanced by mixing it with gerontology. A nice feature of careers in marketing is that many entry-level positions are open to persons with bachelor's degrees, as well as master's in business administration (MBA) degrees. Among the jobs open for professionals with a combined background in marketing and gerontology are the following:

- Market analyst on goods and services targeted at older adult population for a corporation
- Marketing director for a retirement community, long-term care facility, or healthcare corporation
- Marketing coordinator for a consortium of senior centers
- Marketing director for a gerontology professional organization

Relevant professional organizations and Web sites:

- American Marketing Association (AMA): www.marketingpower.com
- Business Forum on Aging (BFA), American Society on Aging (ASA): www.asaging.org

PHILOSOPHY

As with most disciplines, philosophy is a field of study that opens the door of employment for academic professors, theorists, and researchers. With a rising interest among current elders to find meaning in their lives through thoughtful and spiritual endeavors that are beyond or different than religion, there has been a parallel interest in philosophy. Concurrently, there also seems to be movement toward incorporating (or reincorporating) two philosophical approaches, ethics and gerotranscendence, into gerontological professional practice, especially in medical and long-term care settings. Codes of ethics are common in many, if not most, professional organizations. As can be seen in several of the earlier career position profiles, adherence to a code of ethics is a requirement for many professional certifications, registries, and licensure processes. Gerotranscendence is a way of thinking about later life that seems to have roots in geropsychology, philosophy, life course development, and gerontology. Researchers in Sweden and Denmark found evidence of gerotranscendence in older patients and nursing staff reported it to be a helpful way to better understand their elderly and frail patients. Potential professional positions for persons who blend philosophy and gerontology in their programs of student include:

- Multidisciplinary health care team ethicist
- Ethics or gerotranscendence trainer for long-term care and assisted living facility staff members
- Resident ethicist for a long-term care facility
- Philosophy instructor for courses offered through Institutes for Learning in Retirement, Elderhostel, and other older learner programs

Relevant professional organizations and Web sites:

- American Philosophical Association (APA): www.apa.udel.edu
- Association for Practical and Professional Ethics (APPE): www.indiana.edu/~appe

POLITICAL SCIENCE/POLICY AND AGING

Policy, in the form of the Social Security Act and the Older Americans Act, set the stage for gerontology and the formal aging network was created by a marriage between policy and gerontology. Courses on policy and aging are required or strongly recommended for students completing degrees or degree components in gerontology. At least one of the newer doctoral degree programs in gerontology is specific to policy and aging. Positions are open at local (city and county), state, and federal levels for professionals, and the work of the following professionals would be enhanced greatly by adding gerontology to relevant undergraduate and graduate programs of study:

- Legislator
- Legislative aide
- Policy on aging analyst for governmental entities, national and international organizations and associations, and other organizations, agencies, and facilities whose mission is affected by policy and regulatory measures
- Policy on aging advocate for organizations/initiatives for elders

- Policy development consultant for local or county-level boards, commissions, agencies, and facilities that do not have a regular staff position related to policy
- Lobbyist

Relevant professional organizations and Web sites:

- American Political Science Association (APSA): www.apsa.net

RELIGIOUS/SPIRITUAL GERONTOLOGY

In the world of gerontology, religion and spirituality may be related but are not necessarily synonymous. Regardless, there is strong interest in both fields and more gerontology-related professional positions are emerging in a variety of settings, including the following:

- Religious leader for an older adult ministry
- Coordinator of training or gerontology educational consultant/trainer for a faith-based older adult outreach program
- Director of education for a family and older adult programs in a religious center
- Director of spiritual education for a retirement community or long-term care facility
- Gerontology consultant for a spiritual retreat center
- Gerontology educator in a college/university religion department, seminary, or other religion education school or center
- Writer of articles on aging or columnist for a religion-sponsored periodical or other publications

Relevant professional organizations and Web sites:

- Forum on Religion, Spirituality and Aging (FORSA), American Society on Aging (ASA): www.asaging.org
- Formal Interest Group on Religion, Spirituality and Aging, Gerontological Society of America (GSA): www.geron.org

SUBSTANCE ABUSE AND CHEMICAL DEPENDENCY

Older adults are not excluded from the ranks of those who abuse and misuse illegal drugs, prescription and over-the-counter (OTC) drugs, alcohol, and other social drugs. While some elders initiate or become victims of substance abuse and chemical dependency in later life, many enter with poor habits and behaviors begun at earlier life stages. As the population of elders grows over the next two decades or so, it is anticipated that there will be an increased need for professionals to work with elders who have had access to a broader range of drugs of all types and a higher number of persons who enter later life with drug use-related histories already well-established. Gerontological specialists and gerontologists with education and/or training related to substance abuse and chemical dependency will be needed to work with abusive and addicted elders in community-based aging and human service agencies, mental health clinics and facilities, substance abuse rehabilitation treatment centers, counseling programs, and health care facilities in positions such as:

- Substance abuse and chemical dependency prevention educators
- Substance abuse and chemical dependency counselors and therapists
- Substance abuse and chemical dependency rehabilitation specialists
- HIV/AIDS educators and counselors for older adults
- Trainers for professionals and paraprofessionals who work directly with abusive and addicted elders

Relevant professional organizations and Web sites:

- Informal Interest Group on Aging, Alcohol, and Addictions, Gerontological Society of America (GSA): www.geron.org

THEATRE ARTS

"Senior theatre" is theatre for, by, and about older adults and is designed to involve older adults in theatre for recreational and therapeutic purposes. Academic programs and noncredit learning experiences in playwriting, actor training, and technical theatre are offered for undergraduate and graduate theatre arts degree students, older adults who are studying theatre arts, and practitioners currently involved with senior theatre groups. Types of senior theatre productions include standard drama, reader's theatre, musical revues, oral history, and plays based on research about aging and older adults. Possible professional positions for persons with a combined theatre arts and gerontology educational background include:

- Director of a senior theatre program
- Instructor or acting coach for older adults involved with a senior theatre
- Manager or producer for a senior theatre

- Technical theatre director and stage or lighting designer for a senior theatre company
- Consultant to community theatre groups interested in developing a senior theatre
- College/university instructor on senior theatre

Relevant professional organizations and Web sites:

- Association for Theatre in Higher Education (ATHE): www.athe.org
- ATHE Senior Theatre Research and Performance Focus Group: www.athe.org

TRANSPORTATION

One of the major issues that older adults face is in regard to transportation, especially if their ability to drive is limited or restricted due to physical disability, memory loss, medication regimens, financial limitations, or other reasons. The U.S. Department of Transportation has made a major effort over the past few years to focus on the transportation needs and problems of elders in an attempt to find solutions and create more elder-friendly options for transportation at the community level. AARP's "55 and Alive" and similar programs offer refresher driving courses to improve driving skills and outcomes for older drivers. Older driver rehabilitation specialists and programs are in place to help drivers modify and adapt their driving behaviors as age and disability interfere. An entrepreneurial family business is developing a set of "trigger films" (that is, films that are designed to trigger discussion) for use in working with elders and their families and in training professionals. Still, there are more opportunities, including the positions listed below, for gerontological specialists and gerontologists to focus their professional practice on some aspect of transportation for their elderly clients:

- Coordinator of a door-to-door community transportation program for older adults
- Trainer or coordinator of training on aging and driving for law enforcement personnel or medical and mental health professionals
- Gerontology consultant to city or county public transportation department

Relevant professional organizations or Web sites:

- Formal Interest Group on Transportation and Aging, Gerontological Society of America (GSA): www.geron.org

As with the career position profiles and interviews, this listing of career opportunities that are possible as gerontology is linked with academic disciplines and professional fields is intended to give you a sampling and, hopefully, to stimulate your own thinking about even more gerontology career paths and positions that might be a good fit for you. It certainly is not an exhaustive list and many more real and possible positions do exist. Best wishes in your search for your niche in the field of aging and the professional world of gerontology!

Glossary of Acronyms

GERONTOLOGY-SPECIFIC ACRONYMS

AAA	Area Agency on Aging
AAGE	Association for Anthropology and Gerontology
AAGP	American Association for Geriatric Psychiatry
AAHID	American Academy of Healthcare Interior Designers
AAHSA	American Association of Homes and Services for the Aging
AAIA	American Association for International Aging
AARP	AARP (formerly known as American Association for Retired Persons)
AFAR	American Federation of Aging Research
AGE-SW	Association for Gerontology Education in Social Work
AGHD-HBCU	Association for Gerontology and Human Development in Historically Black Colleges and Universities
AGHE	Association for Gerontology in Higher Education
AGS	American Geriatric Society
AIFG	American Institute of Financial Gerontology
AJAS	Association for Jewish Aging Services
ANPPM	Asociacion Nacional Pro Personas Mayores (See NHCOA)
AoA	Administration on Aging
ASA	American Society on Aging
CAPS	Certified Aging-in-Place Specialist
CCGP	Commission for Certification of Geriatric Pharmacists
CCRC	Continuing Care Retirement Community
COA	Commission on Aging (county-level unit on aging)
CPG	Certified Geriatric Pharmacist
CSA	Certified Senior Advisor
FGP	Foster Grandparent Program
GEC	Geriatric Education Center
GCM	National Association of Professional Geriatric Care Managers
GNP	Gerontological Nurse Practitioner
GRCC	Geriatric Research, Education and Clinical Center

GSA	Gerontological Society of America
GU	Generations United
IAGG	International Association of Gerontology and Geriatrics
ICAA	International Council on Active Aging
IFA	International Federation on Ageing
ILC	International Longevity Center
LCOA	Leadership Council of Aging Organizations
LNHA	Licensed Nursing Home Administrator
LTC	Long-term Care
MOWAA	Meals on Wheels Association of America
MCUAAAR	Michigan Center for Urban American Aging Research
NADSA	National Adult Day Services Association
NAELA	National Academy of Elder Law Attorneys
NAFGPD	National Association of Foster Grandparent Program Directors
NAHOF	National Association on HIV Over Fifty
NAIPC	National Aging in Place Council
NANASP	National Association of Nutrition and Aging Services Programs
NAPCA	National Asian Pacific Center on Aging
NARSVPD	National Association of Retired & Senior Volunteer Program Directors
NASCPD	National Association of Senior Companion Project Directors
NASOP	National Association of State Long Term Care Ombudsman Programs
NASUA	National Association of State Units on Aging
NATLA	National Academy for Teaching and Learning about Aging
NCBA	National Caucus and Center on Black Aging
NCEA	National Center on Elder Abuse
NCOA	National Council on Aging
NELF	National Elder Law Foundation
NGNA	National Gerontological Nursing Association
NHCOA	National Hispanic Council on Aging (See ANPPM)
NIA	National Institute on Aging
NICOA	National Indian Council on Aging
NSCLC	National Senior Citizens Law Center
n4a	National Association of Area Agencies on Aging
OAA	Older Americans Act
OWL	Older Women's League
PGCM	Professional Geriatric Care Manager
RFG	Registered Financial Gerontologist

RSVP	Retired Senior Volunteer Program
SAGE	Senior Action in a Gray Environment
SCDA	Special Care Dentistry Association
SCORE	Senior Core of Retired Executives
SCP	Senior Companion Program
SCSEP	Senior Community Service Employment Program

GERONTOLOGY-RELATED ACRONYMS

AA	Alzheimer's Association
AAA	American Academy of Actuaries
AAACE	American Association for Adult and Continuing Education
AAFCS	American Association of Family and Consumer Science
AAHPERD	American Alliance for Health, Physical Education, Recreation & Dance
AAMFT	American Association of Marriage and Family Therapy
AATA	American Art Therapy Association
ACA	American Counseling Association
ACHCA	American College of Health Care Administrators
ACR	Association for Conflict Resolution
ADA	American Dental Association
ADA	American Dietetic Association
ADA	Americans with Disabilities Act
ADEA	Age Discrimination in Employment Act
ADEAR	Alzheimer's Disease Education and Referral Center
ADED	Association for Driver Rehabilitation Specialists
ADTA	American Dance Therapy Association
AFP	Association for Fundraising Professionals
AHTA	American Horticultural Therapy Association
AIA	American Institute of Architects
AICPA	American Institute of Certified Public Accountants
ALA	American Library Association
AMA	American Medical Association
AMTA	American Music Therapy Association
ANA	American Nursing Association
AOA	American Optometric Association
AOTA	American Occupational Therapy Association
APA	American Psychological Association
APHA	American Public Health Association
APPE	Association for Practical and Professional Ethics
APSA	American Political Science Association

APTA	American Physical Therapy Association
ASA	American Sociological Association
ASCP	American Society of Consultant Pharmacists
ASHA	American Speech-Language-Hearing Association
ASID	American Society of Interior Designers
ASSECT	American Association of Sexuality Educators, Counselors & Therapists
ATHE	Association for Theatre in Higher Education
CMS	Centers for Medicare and Medicaid Services
CVAA	Congress of Volunteer Administrators Association
CSWE	Council on Social Work Education
ERISA	Employee Retirement Income Security Act
HAA	Hospice Association of America
HFES	Human Factors and Ergonomics Society
HRSA	Health Resources and Services Administration
MLA	Medical Library Association
NAHB	National Association of Home Builders
NADT	National Association for Drama Therapy
NAHC	National Association for Home Care and Hospice
NASW	National Association of Social Workers
NCCATA	National Coalition of Creative Arts Therapies Associations
NCDA	National Career Development Association
NCFR	National Council on Family Relations
NECA	National Employment Counseling Association
NHF	National Hospice Foundation
NHTSA	National Highway Transportation Safety Administration
NOF	National Osteoporosis Foundation
NRPA	National Recreation and Park Association
NTRS	National Therapeutic Recreation Society
SNE	Society for Nutrition Education
SSA	Social Security Administration